Measuring Spoken Language Proficiency

James R. Frith
Editor

Georgetown University Press, Washington, D.C. 20057

Library of Congress Cataloging in Publication Data

Main entry under title:

Measuring spoken language proficiency.

Papers from a preconference workshop sponsored
by Georgetown University and the Interagency
Language Roundtable and held preceding the 1980
annual Georgetown University Round Table on
Languages and Linguistics.

1. Languages, Modern--Examinations--Congresses.
2. Oral communication--Examinations--Congresses.
I. Frith, James Robert, 1917-   II. Georgetown
University, Washington, D.C. III. United States.
Interagency Language Roundtable.
PB36.F7   407.6   80-20447
ISBN 0-87840-188-1

International Standard Book Number: 0-87840-188-1

CONTENTS

PREFACE

James R. Frith
Foreign Service Institute,
Department of State

The government and the language teaching profession have a great deal to say to each other about foreign language proficiency: how it is gained, how it is lost, how it can be recovered, how it can be measured. Georgetown University and the Interagency Language Roundtable of the federal government have collaborated for several years to provide a forum for such dialog immediately preceding the start of the annual Georgetown University Round Table on Languages and Linguistics. Each year we seek to identify a topic in which language professionals in the government and in the academic world have a mutual and active interest. The topic for this year (and for the 1981 Pre-Conference Workshop) is the measurement of oral proficiency.

Language testing has been emerging in recent time as a major concern in American education. The A, B, C grades which are customarily given at the end of language courses have little meaning beyond the edge of the school ground or the campus. When students venture abroad and have trouble understanding and being understood after high school or college language study, they wonder if those A, B, C grades were some kind of cover-up. Language faculties are confronted with a credibility problem and are increasingly looking for alternatives or supplements to the traditional grading systems, for ways to measure language skills in terms of practical utility.

Three out of five Modern Language Association/American Council of Learned Societies (MLA/ACLS) Task Forces of 1977 and 1978 gave prominent attention to language testing. The first recommendation of the Task Force on the Commonly Taught Languages was that the profession 'should develop an outline of realistic proficiency goals by stage of achievement'. Their recommendation was echoed by the Task Force on the Less Commonly Taught Languages.

The Task Force on Institutional Policy said that one of the 'main sources for dissatisfaction with the present status of language study [is] a failure of the language teaching profession itself to direct its collective energies toward definable goals'. Their report stresses the need for clearly identified competency or proficiency standards and expresses the view

that foreign language study especially lends itself to a universal system of performance evaluation and assessment. In the long run such a system will contribute to the improvement of instruction and curriculum as well as help to restore public confidence in the educational institutions and in the capability of faculty to provide competent language instruction.

The United States government, involved in foreign affairs on a vastly wider front in the post-World War II period than ever before, had to find ways to describe the language requirements of jobs and to measure the language proficiency of prospective incumbents. A set of descriptive statements of language proficiency levels evolved at the Foreign Service Institute in the early 1950s along with a system for assessing proficiency. The descriptions and their short titles (S-1, S-2, etc.) are now commonly used and understood within the government and are a part of the jargon in the papers presented here.

The Foreign Service Institute and other agencies of the United States and Canadian governments welcome the opportunity to share their experience in measuring oral proficiency. We have made a start in a field which leaves much yet to be explored. We believe that the attention of academic colleagues will help to find ways to streamline and otherwise improve the testing procedures now in use in the two governments. We have learned that language performance can be measured with consistent and accurate results. We believe that widely recognized proficiency standards would make it possible for students to set definable proficiency goals and that clear goals will encourage them to continue in language study until they have achieved a useful proficiency.

FIVE COOCCURRING FACTORS
IN SPEAKING PROFICIENCY

Marianne Lehr Adams
Foreign Service Institute,
Department of State

The Foreign Service Institute Oral Interview test of speaking proficiency takes five factors into account, but the evaluation is stated as a single global score (e.g. S-2). It is, of course, possible to identify each factor and one might even devise separate tests for some of the factors. In the FSI Oral Interview test, however, they are observed only as they cooccur in more or less natural conversation. They are resolved into one of 11 possible global speaking (S-) scores ranging from S-0 (no ability) to S-5 (educated native-speaker proficiency). The total list of possible scores is 0, 0+, 1, 1+, 2, 2+, 3, 3+, 4, 4+, 5.

It has been standard practice among experienced FSI testers at the conclusion of oral interview tests to record the global score first and then to record the value placed on each of the factors to explain the global score. (This procedure is not recommended for inexperienced testers.) Thus the global scores given by FSI testers, while being based on definable and observable aspects of linguistic behavior, are not arrived at by a strict sum-of-the-parts methodology. It is instructive, therefore, to examine the values which FSI testers have placed on the five cooccurring factors which they observe in evaluating oral proficiency.

The factors identified for evaluation are accent, comprehension,[1] fluency, grammar, and vocabulary. FSI testers grade the factors on a worksheet which has the following six-point semantic-differential scale.

Accent	foreign	__ __ : __ __ : __ __	native
Comprehension	incomplete	__ __ : __ __ : __ __	complete
Fluency	uneven	__ __ : __ __ : __ __	even
Grammar	inaccurate	__ __ : __ __ : __ __	accurate
Vocabulary	inadequate	__ __ : __ __ : __ __	adequate

1

We sought to find out how the five factors relate to the global speaking score (the S- rating). More explicitly, the question was how the factors differed in value between contiguous S-ratings. In terms of student aspiration, the question was which factors are most critical in improving performance from one level to the next.

In search of answers, we tabulated the factor values shown on the worksheets of 834 tests given during the summer of 1978. This sample included tests in 33 languages (Table 1) and reflected a standard bell-curve distribution (Table 2). The clientele included employees and spouses from all the principal foreign affairs agencies of the government. The tabulations were subjected to discriminant analysis of contiguous ratings via the SPSS program (i.e. Statistical Package for the Social Sciences).

Table 1. Languages represented by 834 Oral Interview tests.

Language	Number	Percent
French	341	41
Spanish	126	15
German	75	9
Russian	50	6
Italian	42	5
Japanese	25	3
Other languages*	175	21

*Afrikaans, Amharic, Burmese, Cambodian, Chinese, Czech, Danish, Dari, Dutch, Farsi, Finnish, Hebrew, Hindi, Hungarian, Indonesian, Korean, Lao, Malay, Nepali, Philipino/Tagalog, Portuguese, Romanian, Serbo-Croatian, Swedish, Tamil, Thai, Urdu.

Table 2. Distribution of speaking scores in 834 tests.

Speaking score	Number	Percent
0 or 0+	7	.8
1	47	5.6
1+	59	7.1
2	97	11.6
2+	169	20.3
3	184	22.1
3+	167	20.1
4	72	8.6
4+	31	3.7
5	1	.1

Discriminant analysis is a procedure to determine which of the factors best characterize two (or more) groups of cases. It does this in a series of steps selecting the most successful discriminator each time. The method used is Wilks' Lambda and the Mahalanobis distance (difference squared) between two groups. These are translated to F ratios for ease of interpretation. At each step one factor is selected, and its significance is stated.

In addition, each previously selected factor is reviewed at every step to see if the information it provided as a single factor is now contained in a combination of factors. If a factor turns out to be redundant, it is removed from the list of significant factors.

This study reports the factors which were found to discriminate between contiguous S ratings with their associated F as well as those factors which do not discriminate. Both pieces of information are useful for interpretation.

The results are interesting from several points of view. In general terms, no factor was removed for redundancy; in other words, all of the factors are operative. The factors which discriminate at each level are given in Table 3; those which do not are given in Table 4. The contiguous levels differ from one another with regard to certain factors, and they are alike with regard to others.

The most consistent difference between S-0+ and S-1 is vocabulary. A person rated S-1 usually has more words at his/her disposal than a person rated S-0+. A person rated S-1+ is usually more fluent than a person rated S-1 but also exceeds the lower level person in comprehension, grammar, and vocabulary. A person rated S-2 comprehends better than a person rated S-1+ and also exceeds him/her in grammar, accent, and fluency. A person rated S-2+ exceeds a person rated S-2 primarily in fluency but also in comprehension, accent, and vocabulary. The major difference between a person rated S-3 and a person rated S-2+ is emphatically grammar. Grammar at the 2+-3 interval is the best discriminator in the table. Accent, vocabulary, and comprehension also discriminate between these two levels. A person rated S-3+ is distinguished from a person rated S-3 primarily in comprehension but also in fluency and grammar. A person rated S-4 has a broader range of vocabulary than a person rated S-3+ but also has a better accent and better control of grammar. Nothing statistically significant distinguishes an S-4 from an S-4+. Since the sample at this level was small, the results may not be conclusive. There was only one case of an S-5 in the entire sample and therefore analysis at that level could not be attempted.

Of interest also are the similarities in the contiguous levels. A person rated S-0+ is like a person rated S-1 in accent, comprehension, fluency, and grammar. A person rated S-1 typically pronounces approximately as well as a person rated S-1+. A person rated S-1+ typically has as broad a range of vocabulary as a person rated S-2. A person rated S-2 is typically as accurate in the use of grammar as a person rated

Table 3. The most discriminating factors.

Between S-	Factors in descending order of significance	F
0+ - 1	Vocabulary	7.52*
1 - 1+	Fluency	57.36*
	Comprehension	32.06*
	Grammar	21.88*
	Vocabulary	16.73*
1+ - 2	Comprehension	22.64*
	Grammar	12.84*
	Accent	9.78*
	Fluency	7.71*
2 - 2+	Fluency	44.53*
	Comprehension	25.63*
	Accent	18.00*
	Vocabulary	13.85*
2+ - 3	Grammar	127.77*
	Accent	67.43*
	Vocabulary	49.07*
	Comprehension	37.73*
3 - 3+	Comprehension	48.73*
	Fluency	27.55*
	Grammar	18.87*
3+ - 4	Vocabulary	36.52*
	Accent	21.35*
	Grammar	14.86*
4 - 4+	Grammar	3.9
	Vocabulary	2.5

*Significant at .99.
At the 4-4+ interval, grammar discriminates at the .94 level of significance and vocabulary at the .90. These levels are considered insufficient to be included with the others, significant at .99.

S-2+. An S-2+ is typically as fluent as an S-3. Both S-3's and 3+'s pronounce well and have a broad range of vocabulary. S-3+'s and S-4's excel in comprehension and fluency.

The study permits us to put the quantitative differences between proficiency levels into words and to construct models of average performance at each level.[2] An S-1 performance typically consists of words, understandable but badly pronounced, in an incomplete phrase environment; responses may or may not be related to the questions asked. An S-1+ performance comes a little closer to conversation because there are enough words but communication falls short on the other factors.

Table 4. The nondiscriminating factors.

Between S	Factors
0+ - 1	Accent
	Comprehension
	Fluency
	Grammar
1 - 1+	Accent
1+ - 2	Vocabulary
2 - 2+	Grammar
2+ - 3	Fluency
3 - 3+	Accent
	Vocabulary
3+ - 4	Comprehension
	Fluency
4 - 4+	Accent
	Comprehension
	Fluency

An S-2 performance is an actual conversation. It consists of appropriate sentences in response to linguistic stimuli at a rate comfortable for both participants in the conversation. Conversation is limited by lack of grammatical control and lack of words. An S-2+ is typically fluent but limited in linguistic structure. An S-3 performance is, first of all, grammatically accurate. At the S-3 level the individual controls the major features of the language and has the vocabulary necessary for general conversation and special interests. An S-3+ performance is typically close to bilingual with respect to comprehension and fluency but far from being truly bilingual with respect to vocabulary, grammar, and accent. At the S-4 level persons demonstrate a broad range of precisely used words--not, of course, in a memorized speech but in unprepared dialogue. The S-4 is near native in pronunciation and controls grammar almost down to the finest detail.

The study is also useful in accounting for some of the common disappointments with test results. Naive appraisals are sometimes in error because they envision a global score while considering only one or two, the least relevant, factors. Thus some people consider themselves S-2 because their vocabulary is sufficient for conversation, but, in fact, it is the other four factors that make the difference between S-1+ and S-2. Other people rate themselves S-3 because of their fluency, but with regard to this factor S-2+ and S-3 are not distinguished from each other. It is grammar that makes the conspicuous difference between these two levels. Still others consider themselves S-4 because they comprehend everything that native speakers comprehend and because they are as fluent as native speakers. But in these two areas S-3+, S-4, and S-4+ are alike. It is grammar and vocabulary that distinguish among them.

NOTES

I am indebted to Dean James R. Frith of the Foreign Service Institute for editorial assistance, and to Ray Clifford for suggesting discriminant analysis as a procedure and for providing the original impetus as well as the clerical help for the study.

1. For the comprehension factor, it is the *evidence* of it which cooccurs with the other factors of speech. Comprehension is demonstrated by the promptness and appropriateness of rejoinders.

2. This exercise does not consider all possible performance types but rather the most frequent. The possible number of combinations of the five factors is vast, and deviations from the average performance do occur. The exercise is useful and informative in providing a statistically valid characterization of a frequently occurring performance at each proficiency level. In a related paper in this volume, Ray Clifford gives information about the accuracy of predicting a global S score from knowledge of the factors.

ALTERNATIVE METHODS OF ORAL PROFICIENCY ASSESSMENT

Francis A. Cartier
Defense Language Institute,
Foreign Language Center

This paper first describes the Defense Language Institute Foreign Language Center (DLIFLC) Spanish Taped Oral Proficiency Test, then discusses several other approaches to the assessment of speaking skills that have not been widely publicized but which may serve to expand our horizons of oral test development. The opinions expressed here are my own and do not purport to reflect the positions of the Department of Defense, the Department of the Army, or the Defense Language Institute.

That several alternative methods of oral proficiency assessment are needed seems clear to all. First, there are several reasons for wanting to assess oral proficiency. And second, as Ray Clifford and Pardee Lowe point out in their paper elsewhere in this volume, the circumstances and environments of test administration differ and do not always permit the use of a face-to-face interview.

Primarily for the second reason, DLI proposed a project in 1971 to develop a prototype oral proficiency test in Spanish that could be administered anywhere that a language lab existed and scored by a trained rater at another time and location. The contract to develop two alternate, equivalent forms of such a test was awarded to Educational Testing Service in July, 1972 and was completed in September, 1974.

The DLIFLC Taped Oral Proficiency Test (or TOPT) requires six components: a master tape, a test booklet, a blank tape, and a manual for test administrators, plus a scoring manual and a scoring sheet for use by the raters. The stimuli are presented in the test booklet and on the master tape, which runs about one hour. The student's responses are recorded on a blank tape.

The current version has four parts. The first part, which is essentially a vocabulary test, presents the student with 68 pictures which the student must identify. The second part, which is meant to test structure, has 60 items. It presents the student with an incomplete Spanish sentence and a complete English translation. The student responds with the whole Spanish sentence. In the third part, the student must perform in seven different simulated communication situations. The last part consists of four passages in English which the student hears and reads. He then responds to a total of 20 questions in Spanish about the passage which he both hears and reads.

Validation was performed by DLI. We administered both an interview similar to that conducted by the Foreign Service Institute and the Spanish Taped Oral Proficiency Test to 109 students; 43 took Form A of the taped test and 66 took Form B. Validation by DLI was discontinued in 1975, resumed in March, 1977, and was completed in September, 1978.

Correlation with the interview ratings was .74 for Form A and .72 for Form B. Interscorer reliability for Form A was .94 and for Form B, .97. Interscorer reliability for the interviews was also .97.

Form B turned out to be slightly better than Form A in mean item discrimination index and gave a somewhat better spread of scores, with a standard deviation of 18.9 points as compared to 14.5 for Form A. Some minor revisions were later made on the basis of the validation data, but these changes would not be expected to affect the data substantially.

As compared to the interview, the taped test has several advantages and at least three disadvantages. One disadvantage is that the taped test is less personal; the student is talking to a machine and not a live, responding person. It is therefore less flexible than the face-to-face interview in adjusting stimuli to the individual student's ability. This inflexibility also means that, if something goes wrong during administration, it is virtually impossible to adjust for it. However, if the recording equipment is properly maintained, mechanical failures (the major source of administration problems) can be kept to a minimum.

Another disadvantage may be in lower validity. Correlations with interview ratings above .70 are quite respectable, but we always hope for something a bit higher. On the other hand, the validity of the taped test and of the interview itself, against some hypothetically perfect real-life criterion measurement, is unknown. I am sure we would all be happy if it turned out to be .70 for either one.

The advantages of the taped test are several. Training time for administrators (who need not speak Spanish) is very small, and training time for raters is substantially less than for the interview.

It can be given as a group test in a language lab.

It is more standardized and more objective than the interview since every student receives identical stimuli and the scoring system is designed to reduce halo effect and other subjective factors to a minimum.

Scoring can be performed at the most convenient or economical time and location, and since the student's responses are all recorded, they can be rescored, also at convenience.

The most important problem regarding the taped test is the question of how to implement and institutionalize the administration and scoring. In the Department of Defense, questions of administration can be handled fairly easily wherever there is a lab or two tape recorders. However, who and where the scorers will be, who will pay them, and so on, are managerial problems of some magnitude. It takes between 30 and 40 minutes to score a tape. If the tests are given in massive numbers, our present faculty will certainly not have the time to score them. If the test is to be used throughout the armed forces, as intended, some other arrangement would have to be made for scoring.

The Taped Oral Proficiency Test nevertheless holds considerable promise for meeting several specific testing requirements in the Armed Services. We therefore have plans to develop similar tests in Russian, German, Chinese-Mandarin, Korean, and Arabic over the next five years. Each will be developed in two alternate forms.

We believe the general format of this test is a practical compromise between the two major theoretical approaches to the testing problem since it measures both specific and global aspects of oral proficiency. There are many other possible approaches and techniques of which I will mention a few in the hope that they may spark a new idea or two for future development.

During the 1950s, the Air Force ROTC needed a test of briefing ability for AFROTC cadets. The American Institutes for Research contracted to develop the test to AFROTC specifications. The idea of a briefing, of course, is that an officer takes information from tables of data and other sources, organizes the facts, and communicates them orally to people who need the information. The tests consisted of a set of facts (for example, about the aircraft maintenance budget for a fighter group) and an outline into which the information was to be organized. The cadet was given 20 minutes to prepare his notes and then presented his briefing to a panel of raters-- usually senior cadets who had been trained to score the briefing. A scoring sheet was designed which listed each fact, arranged in the order prescribed by the outline. The rater had only to check whether the fact was intelligibly received-- completely accurately, fairly closely, distorted, or omitted. A few points were awarded or subtracted on the basis of manner of presentation, but the total score was determined mainly by whether or not the information was communicated in the same form in which it was provided to the cadet on the instruction sheets. It was therefore essentially a test of accurate

information processing. The cadet was even marked down for
adding comments of his own.

When people talk about tests of oral communication skill, I
often think of that test because many who say they want a
'communication skills' test ignore some of the most essential
aspects of good communication. If your purpose in testing a
foreign service employee, or a member of the armed forces, or
someone else, is to determine whether that person can convey
facts in the foreign language, then it seems to me that some
measure of factual accuracy is mandatory. Furthermore, if the
person is supposed to be able to gather information rather than
give it, or to persuade or convince others, or perform effectively in meetings, then some measure of those communication
skills (and, I presume, some actual skill training) is mandatory.
If you do not test these things, you must not, in my opinion,
claim to be testing communication skills.

In the early 1960s, Paul Heinberg at the University of Hawaii
developed a quite different test in connection with a remedial
instructional system for native Hawaiians and foreign students
who had failed the oral English test that was required of all
graduates of the University of Hawaii. He first observed students taking the University oral performance test before the
panel of judges and analyzed the behavior of the failures. His
front-end analysis (as we would now call it) revealed that the
panel's decisions were often highly subjective but that, for the
most part, five factors seemed to be involved in impressing
those judges. Heinberg's test--a true criterion-referenced test--
was constructed so simply that even fellow students could--and
did--administer and score it reliably. I will describe it as well
as I remember it from my visit to the University of Hawaii about
15 years ago. (Some details may be inaccurate, but I recall
the principle of the test quite clearly.) The individual was required to talk, on any subject, with or without notes, but not
memorized, while meeting the following criteria. First, eye contact must be maintained during all moments of vocalization.
Second, sufficient loudness must be maintained, even to the
last syllable of the sentence, that a person about eight feet
away could hear. Third, articulation must be sufficiently
clear for intelligibility of every word. Fourth, I believe, was
a measure of fluency of some kind, and fifth, there must be
adequate variety of intonation to be judged as expressive
rather than monotonous.

The first part of the test required two minutes of talking,
meeting only the criterion of eye contact, then two minutes
more maintaining eye contact and meeting the loudness criterion
as well, then two minutes meeting those two criteria plus the
intelligibility criterion, and so on. The whole test, with in-
structions, pauses between two-minute segments, etc., required
less than 30 minutes to administer and score. I will not attempt
to explain exactly why it was formatted this way except to say
that the test format was also the format of the main part of the

training program. The student simply took the test over and over under certain behavior modification conditions until he or she passed it. It worked remarkably well. Virtually all the students who passed Heinberg's test, and were thereby certified as ready, also passed the University test in front of the panel. It had excellent concurrent validity, which was Heinberg's sole intent for it.

His inclusion of eye contact as a criterion, for example, resulted from his meticulous observation of the various behaviors that the panel of judges seemed to require, though the judges themselves were not conscious of it as a criterion for passing. Heinberg's test illustrates an important point: subjective factors should not necessarily be ignored and sometimes can be analyzed objectively. Heinberg's approach to test building deserves very careful consideration as we search for new techniques of measuring oral proficiency.

During the Southeast Asian conflict, Sydney Sako and I (then at the DLI English Language Center, Lackland Air Force Base) were assigned to develop an oral proficiency test in Vietnamese. After a few months, the project was set aside for higher priority work and was never finished, but its concept may be of interest since it was a predecessor of the DLI Taped Oral Proficiency Tests. We wanted to be able to measure a broad range of achievement from very simple enabling skills up to a fairly sophisticated ability to communicate facts. Again I am relying on memory.

As I remember it, the test began with several recorded sentences, each incorporating one or two essential phonological features, such as a particular tone, critical to the meaning. The student merely repeated the sentence aloud onto a blank tape. Like all other item types in the test, the first items were easy and following items became progressively more difficult. These mimicry items were followed by some questions on tape, in Vietnamese, which the student answered, and then some sentences in English to be interpreted into Vietnamese, each presenting a special grammatical problem.

The next part consisted of a single item: a picture of an ordinary office pencil sharpener. The student was asked to tell what it was and how to use it. This was intended to simulate the problem of explaining a mechanical device to Vietnamese military personnel. The next-to-last part was a simulated phone call which required the student to carry on a sort of conversation with a tape-recorded voice which was identified as a Vietnamese colonel. And the last item was a fairly complex drawing of combat activity which the student was asked to describe in a simulated radio report to a Vietnamese unit commander.

We administered this test to about 100 students and asked three Vietnamese instructors to rate the tapes according to a carefully designed rating sheet. For example, in the first part --the sentence mimicry items--they rated only the student's pronunciation of one or two specified words. This resulted in fairly high inter-rater reliability.

An unexpected and interesting thing occurred while Mr. Sako and I were observing the three raters work. We were playing the student tapes for them on a loudspeaker and, just to keep from getting bored, Sako and I, neither knowing any Vietnamese, picked up scoring sheets and began to rate the students ourselves. Later, we compared our ratings with those of the Vietnamese instructors and found a substantial correlation. When we discovered that, we wished we had gone about it more seriously and had made careful notes of what we were doing. We speculated that our judgments were made primarily on the basis of our perceptions of concomitant variables, such as a student's reaction time between stimulus and response, number and type of disfluencies, perceived confidence, and things like that.

One completely objective factor was a student's total omission of a response to a particular item. Since the items were designed to progress from easy to difficult in each part, and from part to part, item omission rate increased as the test progressed and was, in fact, a significant factor that was easily measured even without knowledge of Vietnamese.

This was done with no scientific intent, but it indirectly confirmed an idea that had arisen earlier in connection with a theoretical problem we had set for ourselves: how does one develop a machine-scorable test of oral proficiency? Our idea was that there must be a number of concomitant variables to oral proficiency that could be measured in a machine-scorable test battery. If we could find several such variables, each of which correlated even a little bit with oral proficiency, but which did not correlate too highly with each other, perhaps the overall multiple correlation would have sufficiently high concomitant validity with a more direct test, such as the FSI interview, to make it a useful measurement where trained interviewers were not available.

This led us to a project we called the Indirect Measure of Oral Proficiency (IMOP). This was another of those ill-fated projects that was curtailed because of other priorities, but we got as far as contracting for a start on it. Jesse Villareal, a speech pathologist and phonetician, was then chairman of the Speech Department at the University of Texas, Austin, and was also working with the University's program in English as a Foreign Language. From his observations of foreign students, he concluded that one ability that improved in proportion to their oral proficiency was the ability to detect whether another person had learned English as a second language or was a native speaker, regardless of the native speaker's regional dialect or other idiosyncracies. It was an odd idea, but Villareal has both curiosity and courage. He made up a 50-item test consisting of 25 sentences spoken spontaneously by nonnative speakers of English, and 25 spoken by native speakers from various regions, minorities, socioeconomic levels, and so on. Each set of 25 sentences ranged from very poor to very good spoken English. He tested only about 30 foreign students at the University of Texas and Lackland Air Force Base, who ranged (on the basis of their instructor's ratings) from poor to very good in spoken English. The test consisted of making only a binary decision for each item: is this a native or a nonnative speaker of English? As I recall, Villareal got a positive rank-order correlation approaching .40, which looked very promising, considering the low number and that the test gave a very limited range of scores, mostly at the high end. In my opinion, we might have achieved .45 or better with a revised version and a better criterion metric. Now, a .45 predictive validity is quite insufficient by itself, but Sydney Sako and I hypothesized that four or five other machine-scorable factors might be found which, when added together in a battery, would predict oral proficiency well enough to serve the particular screening and placement purposes we had in mind.

It is customary in such cases to comment that more research is needed, which is true; but to develop a machine-scorable test of oral proficiency, we first need some thinking (consciously and deliberately creative thinking, at least as imaginative as Jesse Villareal's) to come up with hypotheses about other possible concomitant variables. If you believe it cannot be done, then it cannot be done. I believe it can be done, if we can find some more Jesse Villareals. Perhaps there are some among the readers of this paper.

Another unusual test that intrigues me is now under development by Joseph Lyons, Professor of Psychology, University of California at Davis. His test, which is based on Claude Shannon's mathematical theory of communications, requires the student to guess each successive letter in a series of sentences. It uses a chemical 'magic answer sheet' that tells the student (by the color raised on the sheet by a chemical felt pen) when he has guessed wrong or right. So, for example, when he is guessing the fourth letter, he knows what the first three letters actually are. Data collected so far shows that error rate on his test discriminates between native and nonnative speakers of English and also of Spanish. His proposal for further validation is the most interesting part of his February 27, 1980, letter.

We plan to select approximately 30 speakers of some non-English language, whose skills span the range of competence from beginner to native, and to videotape them in interaction with native speakers of the language in a wide variety of simulated situations. In each situation, the native speakers will serve as spontaneously behaving participants, and the test subjects will be placed in the situations and left free to cope. Their performances will then be judged by skilled interviewers, using rating techniques such as those used in the State Department's oral interview method. From the profile of scores thus obtained, we will develop regression equations so as to predict real-life skills from scores on our measure. We anticipate that the program will call for about 150 half-hour videotapes, made by a professional crew over a period of 18 months.

Lyons' test is not exactly machine-scorable, but it comes close. In any case, his approach to validation is well worth pondering.

It may be useful, in conclusion, to append a few comments on hang-ups regarding language tests and to make one recommendation. There are several conflicts and misunderstandings that seem to be hindering our progress, including debates about testing competence versus performance, achievement versus proficiency, the relative value of seeking content, construct, or predictive validity (and of face validity, too), preference for norm-referenced testing or for criterion-referenced testing, or criterion-scored norm-referenced testing, or whatever. I would like to introduce a new concept: decision-referenced testing. Many of the arguments we hear and read are between people who do not realize they are arguing about totally different decisions. Some people are primarily interested in tests that will help them manage an instructional process, while others want tests they can use to help them make personnel assignment decisions. Another group of test makers is less interested in either of these practical problems than in proving or disproving various hypotheses about language learning or testing, that is, in 'doing science'. This is by no means an exhaustive list of the various perspectives which, unfortunately, tend to be lumped together indiscriminately.

What each of us must do--but too often neglects--is identify, in precise language, the type of decision that is to be made, and build the particular type of test that will provide the optimum data to guide that particular decision. I recommend the perspective of 'decision-referenced testing' and call your attention to Schneider's Law: 'Be careful what you want; you may get it'.

TOWARD A COMMON MEASURE OF SPEAKING PROFICIENCY

John L. D. Clark
Educational Testing Service

I have been asked to discuss some of the considerations that would seem to be involved in the development and use of a 'common measure' of speaking proficiency in second or foreign languages. A 'common measure', as I propose to use the term, refers to a uniform testing procedure that could be used with diverse groups of examinees in a variety of language-learning and language-use situations, with testing results reported on a single uniform scale.

The 'common measure' approach can be contrasted to the rationale and the development procedure underlying the preparation of speaking tests for specialized and closely predefined purposes, as, for example, the job-specific testing protocols recently developed for the Ottawa civil service (Mareschal 1980) and the generally similar testing approaches being followed by the English Language Consultancy Department of the British Council (B. J. Carroll 1978). In the latter two instances and in other comparable projects, considerable attention is focused on analyzing, in the greatest possible detail, the specific linguistic demands of a particular employment situation or other predefined language use context; following this detailed analysis, a highly individualized speaking test is developed, in which are featured the particular lexical items, structural elements, and modes of discourse most functionally related to the specific language-use situation in question.

I certainly have no theoretical quarrel with such an approach. Indeed, for those situations in which it is financially and administratively feasible to devote the amount of effort required to conduct a detailed language-use analysis, the resulting test instruments would, in all probability, be at least somewhat more closely related to (and hence, better predictors of) those particular linguistic performances involved in the specified applications than would a more generalized instrument. However, from a number of other standpoints, there seems to be considerable justification in urging the development of a more generally applicable measure of speaking proficiency that could be used with confidence and with pragmatically useful results in the large number of situations for which tailor-made assessment procedures are not a realistic possibility.

The preparation, validation, and subsequent practical use of such a 'common measure' test of speaking ability would involve five major steps. Each of these would be a considerable undertaking in its own right, but all would be required in order to properly develop and implement the common measure approach. In chronological order, the five steps are as follows: (1) development of an extensive battery of experimental test formats, (2) development of an extensive battery of experimental criterion measures, (3) large-scale administration of test formats and criterion measures, (4) specification of final test formats and criterion measures, (5) cross-validation and norming of final 'common measure' test. Each of these steps and their operational interrelationships are described in greater detail in the following paragraphs.

1. **Development of an extensive battery of experimental test formats.** As a largely inexact science (at least at the present state of development of the discipline), foreign- and second-language proficiency testing does not enjoy the detailed logical and theoretical frameworks within which research and development activities take place in the 'hard' sciences. More simply stated, although a certain amount of useful work in the area of 'communicative competence' has already taken place (Savignon 1972; Canale and Swain 1979), there is at present no uniform or widely agreed-upon theoretical structure to guide the specification and development of testing procedures intended to measure this competence objectively.

In the absence or near absence of comprehensive conceptual guidelines for the test development process, it is suggested that the most appropriate procedure for instrument development would be to submit to empirical tryout a large number of potentially useful assessment formats, including not only those that might be derived from presently available theoretical discussions of communicative proficiency, but also various tried and (presumed) true procedures that have been found to serve well in other testing contexts, as well as a number of new, experimental possibilities that would appear to hold some measurement promise.

Thus, the suggested first step in the common measure test development process would be to convene a number of professional language testers, psycholinguists concerned with measurement problems, and others familiar with the technical and linguistic considerations at issue, for whom the common goal would be to propose, discuss, and come to general agreement on a large number of prospective formats to be included in a quite lengthy, experimentally oriented testing battery. It would be expected that peer review and discussion in the course of this initial activity would eliminate from consideration any proposed testing procedures that are seen to have serious theoretical or practical shortcomings, but would at the same time allow sufficient latitude to include any suggested formats that would seem to have reasonable prospects of contributing to the measurement potential of the total battery.

Without intending to prejudge the final outcome of this process in any way (and, indeed, reflecting only one person's possibly idiosyncratic views), I would suggest that face-to-face conversation along the general lines of the Foreign Service Institute interview procedure (see Clark 1972, Wilds 1975, Sollenberger 1978) would be expected to constitute one important component of the total battery. The basic rationale for this suggestion is the great psychometric advantage available in the FSI interview format (and other face-to-face conversational settings) of being able to modify, on a moment-by-moment basis, the pacing, scope, and level of interviewer-examinee interaction so as to maximize the amount of useful information being obtained at any given point in the testing process. This possibility is, of course, not available in the fixed and predetermined format of booklet- and/or tape recording-mediated speaking tests (Clark 1979). The representational validity of the interviewing process as a reasonably close approximation, if not absolutely realistic reflection, of real-life conversational settings would also favor the inclusion of a face-to-face interaction between examinee and tester as one component of the complete battery.

On the other hand, certain inherent limitations of the conversational format would appear to make advisable the inclusion of a number of other assessment techniques in the complete experimental battery. Lado (1978) has cited, among others, the problem of adequate sampling of lexicon in the course of the usual FSI-type interview. The number of topical areas that can be broached in the course of a 15-20 minute conversation is relatively limited by comparison to the depth and range of lexical control that would be expected of examinees at, say, FSI Level 2+ and above, and the 'luck of the draw' with respect to the topics actually discussed during any given interview may unfairly aid or disadvantage the examinee involved.

A number of different testing formats could be proposed to probe lexical control more widely and more effectively, including, for example, presenting a number of line drawings or photographs depicting various objects and asking the examinee to identify the objects portrayed. A series of such pictures, carefully selected to include not only the most common objects but also much less frequently encountered items (all of which, however, would be within the general experience of the average native speaker), would provide detailed vocabulary-related data

that cannot usually be obtained in the ordinary course of the
FSI-type interview.

With regard to grammatical control, experienced FSI interviewers are usually quite adept at eliciting basic verb tenses
and other common morphological and syntactic features of the
test language. Again, however, there are frequent instances
in which it is not realistically possible to verify examinee control of more sophisticated grammatical elements (such as com-
pound past tenses or various uses of the subjunctive in French)
while maintaining a reasonable semblance of natural conversation. Although severely criticized as a testing procedure by
Brooks (1964) and other strict adherents to the audiolingual
tenets of the early sixties, the straightforward oral translation,
from native language into the test language, of lexically simple
phrases embodying the particular grammatical structures at
issue would seem a useful complement to the basic conversational format and could provide a more objective and more comprehensive assessment of this area of performance than would
the conversational segment alone.

A third area in which additional testing techniques could use-
fully be introduced into the total experimental battery involves
the examinee's ability to convey appropriate 'affect' through the
selection of suitable register, lexicon, and intonation patterns.
This important aspect of communicative proficiency might be
very effectively addressed, for example, by asking the examinee
to convey a series of messages in specified interpersonal situations. One such instruction to the examinee might be to 'pre-
tend that I am an obnoxious door-to-door salesman, and tell me
in no uncertain terms that you do not have the slightest inten-
tion of buying anything from me'. In carrying out this portion
of the test, the examiner would present several predetermined
situation/message combinations, increasing in sophistication from
the most basic expressions of affect (e.g. anger, great in-
credulity) up to the more subtle expressions of irony, appropriate verbal deference to authority, and so forth.

In the interview setting, the examinee's competence in those
aspects of 'listening comprehension' associated with oral interaction is not as thoroughly measured as it could be through
the use of other supplementary techniques. Tape recordings
or perhaps even videotapes could be used to present spoken
stimuli drawn from a considerably greater number of communicative situations than can be effectively presented in a conversational setting with a single interlocutor; these could include
speakers with regional accents, children's voices, and even
speech in less than optimum acoustic conditions, such as typical
'cocktail party' talk and conversations over a faulty telephone
connection.

Within the large-scale test battery, there should also be pro-
vision for trying out a number of more highly experimental
testing techniques. Although in many cases these techniques
would have relatively little face validity as reflections of

real-life language use, they could be anticipated to correlate at a quite high level with the external criterion measures to be used in the validation study. As such, these experimental formats could quite legitimately be included in a prototype 'common measure' speaking test along with the more widely used techniques. One example of an experimental format would be the verbatim repetition, by the examinee, of heard sentences of increasing length and complexity, as investigated by Clark and Swinton (1979) in connection with the development of an English-second-language speaking test for the Teachers of English as a Foreign Language program. Many other experimental testing procedures could be proposed, either derived from specific hypotheses concerning the psycholinguistic components of 'speaking proficiency' or having a more serendipitous ('why don't we try ...') origin.

The basic intent of the preceding discussion is not to suggest that the few examples shown are fully representative of the formats and procedures that might be included in the prototype test battery, or even that these would prove to be the most useful formats, but simply to emphasize that it would be highly desirable, as the first step in the creation and validation of a truly comprehensive testing instrument, to specify and develop these and a variety of other testing formats--based on the best thinking of a number of interested researchers--to provide the initial measurement corpus from which the specific content and procedures for the common measure would ultimately be drawn.

2. **Development of an extensive battery of experimental criterion measures.** Although the planning and development of a substantial battery of prototype speaking test formats would be a major undertaking in its own right, this accomplishment would not of itself be of real value from technical, psychometric, or practical-use standpoints unless and until an equally painstaking validation study had been carried out, in which the testing results of wide-scale administration of the proposed formats had been statistically related to suitable criterion measures of speaking proficiency in actual communicative situations.

This requirement poses a major theoretical and practical problem in the development of the common measure instrument because there do not exist, at the present time, any sufficiently accurate or extensive criterion measures of real-life communicative performance against which the common measure test could be appropriately validated.

Until fairly recently, my own thinking with regard to the 'criterion problem' had been oriented toward conceptualizing and developing very complex and detailed simulations of real-life language-use situations and observing the examinee's performance in these situations. Those of us who have attempted to set up realistic communicative situations in a direct testing context are aware of the very great number of practical complexities that must be faced in arranging testing contingencies that are even minimally reflective of the real-life settings in which the actual linguistic performances take place. A testing room can never be adequately outfitted so as to incorporate, in a highly realistic manner, the physical setting of a restaurant, railway station, or other specified language-use site, and to the extent that the physical setting has any bearing on the nature of the communicative activity (e.g. the possibility of pointing to desired items in a shop as an aid in communication), the face and content validity of the simulated situation are correspondingly reduced.

By the same token, the examiner in his or her role as test administrator cannot usually provide the detailed and subtle role-related cues that are present in the 'genuine' communicative setting. As Perren (1967) has expressed it:

> ... both participants know perfectly well that it is a test and not a tea-party, and both are subject to psychological tensions, and what is more important, to linguistic constraints of style and register thought appropriate to the occasion by both participants.

These and a variety of other difficulties in attempting to approximate real-life situations for criterion testing purposes would appear to make the investigation of alternative approaches to the criterion measurement problem highly desirable and, in all probability, inevitable if this problem is to be satisfactorily resolved. Two possible approaches, which I feel merit much more intensive discussion, development, and analysis than have been accorded them to date, are, first, the use of detailed examinee self-report data with respect to speaking proficiency and, second, independent ('second-party') evaluation of speaking performance in 'on-the-job' situations.

With regard to self-report data, there would appear to be a real wealth of perceptive and detailed information about language competence in the mind of the second-language learner/user-- information which could be obtained in a thoroughgoing and reliable way if only sufficiently sensitive and detailed questionnaire instruments could be developed for this purpose. In this respect, a number of useful attempts have already been made, including the student questionnaires used in a parametric study of second language learning by Peace Corps volunteers (Carroll et al. 1966) and an extensive proficiency self-appraisal instrument developed by the Experiment in International Living (1976).

A recent ETS study has involved the development of a series of 'can do' questionnaire statements concerning the respondent's ability to use the language for each of a number of specified 'real-life' purposes (for example, 'say the days of the week', 'buy clothes in a department store', 'talk about my favorite hobby at some length, using appropriate vocabulary'). These items have been found to correlate at a level of about .60-.65

with actual speaking proficiency as measured by the FSI technique. Correlations of this magnitude are encouraging, and there is reason to believe that further refinement of the specific questions asked, together with the use of differential weighting techniques, would raise these correlations substantially.
As a further consideration, it should be noted that there is no reason to assume that the lack of higher correlation at the present time is attributable exclusively or even predominantly to the self-assessment measures, and it is reasonable to assume that further refinement of the direct testing measures themselves along the lines discussed in the preceding section would also help to produce a considerably closer relationship between these two types of measures.

The second, largely parallel, approach to the criterion measure problem would be to obtain 'on-the-job' appraisals of language performance from persons other than the examinee who are in a position to observe this performance in an extensive and detailed way, for example: the department chairmen (or even the classroom students) of nonnative teaching assistants in a college teaching context; the first-line supervisors of civil service workers; and so forth. It would be important to insure that the language-use questions posed would be readily understandable to nonspecialist respondents and as free as possible from extraneous influences, but this could be accomplished through appropriate clinical trials of the questionnaire materials, as well as through careful analysis of the large-scale validation study results.

In summary of the foregoing discussion, it is suggested that one useful approach to the development of suitable criterion measures against which to compare the results of a comprehensive common measure speaking test would be to prepare a large corpus of questionnaire-based self- and second-party language proficiency assessment materials which, like the proposed direct measures themselves, would be based on the best thinking and joint efforts of a number of test developers and language researchers involved in the common measure project. These materials would include potentially useful items from existing questionnaires, as well as a large number of newly prepared questions--desirably involving the use of 'can-do' statements of language proficiency--from which the most effective subsets of questions would be drawn based on the results of the large-scale experimental administration.

3. **Large-scale administration of test formats and criterion measures.** It would be difficult to specify at this juncture the amount of testing time that would be needed to administer both the experimental direct testing measures and the extensive questionnaire materials intended to provide the necessary criterion data. As a rough approximation, at least one full day of examinee time would probably be required to complete all the direct tests and self-report questionnaire items, with an

additional one to two hours for questionnaire completion by
second-party evaluators.

As previously discussed, the strategy for development of the
common measure instrument would be to select an operational
subset of testing formats from the larger battery of experimental measures, based on the statistical results of the simul-
taneous administration of the test battery and criterion
questionnaire materials to a large sample of examinees. In
order for the operational test to serve adequately as a 'common
measure' of speaking proficiency in a wide variety of language-
use situations, it would be important to include, in the test
administration sample, students and other language learners/
users drawn from as many as possible of the examinee populations of interest.

It is not possible at this point to provide a detailed inven-
tory of the kinds of examinee groups that should be included
in the administration sample. However, by way of example,
possible groups include any and all of the following: (1) students in regular school-based language programs, junior high
school through college; (2) a wide range of persons using
foreign languages in on-the-job situations, including tour
guides, office workers whose job involves spoken interaction
in the test language, Peace Corps volunteers, and members of
other service-abroad organizations; (3) language teachers at
all academic levels; (4) residents and tourists abroad; and (5)
self-learners and other individuals who have acquired competence in a second language through social exposure and daily
living contacts rather than through formal instruction.

Three important advantages are associated with obtaining the
widest possible initial administration sample. First, this would
help insure an adequately wide range of examinee performance
on the test formats. Second, administering the prototype test
materials to a diverse sample of examinees would help to point
out particular item formats or other aspects of the testing procedure which appear to be biased toward or against a particular group of examinees. For example, some parts of the experimental test battery might make use of a procedure to which
the academic students have been frequently exposed but that
would be much less familiar to nonacademic examinees. In this
and other similar situations, statistical comparisons across
groups, together with clinical debriefing of the examinees
concerning their thoughts and reactions in working through
the various sections of the test, would help to identify any
problems of this type.

Third, on the assumption that each of the examinee sub-
groups for the administration would complete--in addition to
the more general questions--a number of items concerning
their ability to use the language appropriately in their particular areas of language use, the initial test administration
could serve as a 'first pass' at developing normative information relating test scores to self-appraised (or second-party

evaluated) language competence in both general and special-purpose situations. Although this type of information would become available in a more systematic and more directly usable form following the cross-validation administration of the completed common measure test, the general outline of these normative correspondences could be examined as part and parcel of the initial administration of the larger battery of prospective test formats.

It should be understood, of course, that more than a single test/questionnaire administration session would probably be required to gather the necessary data from the large number of examinee groups involved. However, if these administrations were conducted under generally identical conditions, data from each administration could be legitimately pooled in a single analysis matrix.

4. Specification of final test formats and criterion measures. Analysis of the test administration results would be expected to involve, in addition to the use of standard item analysis techniques, examination of zero-order correlations relating each of the component sections of the prototype speaking test (i.e. each of the various item formats) to each other and to the numerous criterion variables available in the self-appraisal and second-party appraisal questionnaires. Appropriate additional analyses cannot be fully specified at this point, but these would probably include factor analytic techniques and canonical correlation studies for various configurations of predictor and criterion variables.

In addition to the statistical analyses per se, examinee reactions to and comments concerning the test formats and questionnaire materials, as well as a variety of practical considerations, would enter into the final content decisions for both the criterion questionnaires and the common measure test. Total testing time for the final version of the common measure instrument would be estimated as about one to two hours--probably too long for routine, wide-scale use. However, a test of this length could quite reasonably be used for 'important' testing decisions, involving such matters as offers of employment, certification of satisfactory completion of a lengthy program of studies, and so forth.

5. Cross-validation and norming of final 'common measure' test. The large-scale test administration process I have described would have identified a subset of test formats that collectively (and possibly with some postadministration revisions) would constitute the final common measure instrument. In order to cross-validate the completed test with a new sample of examinees and to develop criterion-related norming information based on the common measure test in its established operational form, the final step in the development process would be to administer the common measure test, along with the

(similarly refined) criterion questionnaires, to new groups of examinees representing the measurement populations of interest. Based directly on this second administration cycle, it would be possible to develop extremely useful interpretive information relating scores on the common measure test to questionnaire-based statements of language proficiency. Such information could be presented in readily understandable ways, for example, in expectancy tables permitting such interpretations as

for a score of X on the common measure speaking test, Y percent of the examinees in Z norming group considered themselves able to 'state and support with examples and reasons a position on a controversial topic (for example, birth control, nuclear safety, environmental pollution)'.

Similar information derived from second-party criterion data could be of the form 'for a score of A on the common measure speaking test, B percent of the examinees in C norming group were considered able to "carry out all of their normal employment functions" using the test language'.

Users of the test results could consult the most suitable expectancy tables for the particular real-life situations in question or--if sufficiently relevant norming data were not available--could develop more appropriate data based on further administration of the common measure test, together with suitably adapted self-rating and/or second-party questionnaires, to the new examinee group of interest. The common measure test could also be used in more traditional prediction contexts in which the criterion of interest could be, for example, successful completion of a specialized language training program as a function of various initial test scores on entry into the program.

An important service that could be provided to users of the common measure test--and assuming that an appropriate administrative structure could be arranged--would be to establish a clearinghouse for reports of additional norming administrations, further research studies, and other information concerning the test and its applications; through this kind of regularized information sharing, the utility (and utilization) of the common measure test could be maximized, consistent with constantly making available the most up-to-date information regarding its appropriate uses and the proper interpretation of the testing results.

Conclusions. It appears that the bulk of this paper has described the possible development and empirical validation of a comprehensive 'common measure' test of speaking proficiency, leaving only a few minutes to emphasize the potential value of carrying out such a project. I believe that there are at least three important reasons why an undertaking of this magnitude should be very strongly considered. First is the inherent interest and challenge of the research endeavor itself. We know, as language testers and as users of testing results, that we have not yet pushed the test development process to anywhere near its maximum potential. To the extent that we can envision even more sophisticated, even more highly informational assessment procedures, we would be selling ourselves short not to attempt to advance our measurement technology beyond its present levels, quite purely and simply as a matter of professional pride and research involvement.

Second, and somewhat more pragmatically, the successful development of a comprehensive 'common measure' proficiency test would make available a highly refined and very powerful assessment instrument which could be used, in its own right, to evaluate communicative proficiency in situations for which the use of such an instrument would be considered both desirable and time- and cost-effective.

Third would be the opportunity to use the common measure test in research and development studies aimed at validating other kinds of existing and newly developed speaking tests of smaller scope and more amenable to routine administration. Comparison of these latter tests to the comprehensive common measure would establish the extent to which they could appropriately be used as stand-ins for the common measure test and would point out both their strengths and, in some cases, possible measurement limitations. In all instances, the test user would be in a position to evaluate thoroughly the measurement results obtained from these 'smaller-scope' instruments and to give appropriate weight and credence to the information they provide.

REFERENCES

Brooks, Nelson. 1964. Language learning: Theory and practice. 2nd edition. New York: Harcourt, Brace and World.

Canale, Michael, and Merrill Swain. 1979. Theoretical bases of communicative approaches to second language teaching and testing. Toronto: Ontario Institute for Studies in Education.

Carroll, Brendan J. 1978. Specifications for an English language testing service. London: The British Council.

Carroll, John B., John L. D. Clark, Roland J. B. Goddu, Thomas M. Edwards, and Fannie A. Handrick. 1966. A parametric study of language training in the Peace Corps. Cambridge, Mass.: Laboratory for Research in Instruction, Graduate School of Education, Harvard University.

Clark, John L. D. 1972. Foreign language testing: Theory and practice. Philadelphia: Chilton/Center for Curriculum Development.

Clark, John L. D. 1979. Direct vs. semi-direct tests of
    speaking ability. In: Concepts in language testing: Some
    recent studies. Edited by Eugène J. Brière and Frances B.
    Hinofotis. Washington, D.C.: TEFL.
Clark, John L. D., and Spencer S. Swinton. 1979. An
    exploration of speaking proficiency measures in the TOEFL
    context. TOEFL Research Report No. 4. Princeton, N.J.:
    Educational Testing Service.
Experiment in International Living. 1976. Your objectives,
    guidelines and assessment: An evaluation form of communi-
    cative competence. Revised. Brattleboro, Vt.: The
    Experiment in International Living.
Lado, Robert. 1978. Scope and limitations of interview-based
    language testing: Are we asking too much of the interview?
    In: Direct testing of speaking proficiency: Theory and
    application. Edited by John L. D. Clark. Princeton, N.J.:
    Educational Testing Service. 113-128.
Mareschal, Roger. 1980. Evaluating second language oral
    proficiency in the Canadian Government. [This volume,
    40-59.]
Perren, George. 1967. Testing ability in English as a second
    language: 3. Spoken language. English Language Teaching
    22:197-202.
Savignon, Sandra J. 1972. Communicative competence: An
    experiment in foreign-language teaching. Philadelphia:
    Chilton/Center for Curriculum Development.
Sollenberger, Howard E. 1978. Development and current use
    of the FSI Oral Interview Test. In: Direct testing of speak-
    ing proficiency: Theory and application. Edited by
    John L. D. Clark. Princeton, N.J.: Educational Testing
    Service. 1-12.
Wilds, Claudia P. 1975. The oral interview test. In: Test-
    ing language proficiency. Edited by Randall L. Jones and
    Bernard Spolsky. Arlington, Va.: Center for Applied Lin-
    guistics. 29-44.

FOREIGN SERVICE INSTITUTE
FACTOR SCORES AND GLOBAL RATINGS

Ray T. Clifford
Language School,
Central Intelligence Agency

Introduction. It is well known that the Foreign Service Institute oral proficiency rating system assigns global language proficiency scores, but many are surprised to find that FSI raters also evaluate candidates' performance on specific factors thought to contribute to general language performance. The presence of both FSI global ratings and FSI factor scores raises the important research question of whether global ratings are predictable from factor scores on accent, grammar, vocabulary, fluency, and comprehension. Since the answer to this question would have direct implications for oral proficiency testing and rating, it was decided to conduct additional research into the relationship between general language proficiency and skills in contributing language factors.

Procedures. The language proficiency scoring sheets for over 900 FSI tests were used as the data source for the study. These sheets contained both global FSI ratings and factor scores on the five skill categories listed in the preceding paragraph. The factor scores (independent variables) and global ratings (dependent variables) were analyzed, using multiple group discriminant analysis. This statistical procedure was selected because it maximizes the ratio of among-group to within-group dispersion in the discriminant analysis space, that is, it makes the groups to be analyzed as statistically different as possible. Once this is accomplished, prediction equations are computed for determining the most probable group (global rating) for each set of factor scores, and the adequacy of the prediction equations is tested against the global ratings actually assigned.

Findings. The first important finding was that all the FSI factors do, in fact, play a role in general language proficiency. All the factor scores contributed significantly to the discriminant analysis at about the .02 level or better.

Table 1. Univariate and multivariate F values and probabilities.

	Univariate F	Univariate probability	Multivariate F	Multivariate probability
Accent	210.93	0.0	5.76	0.0001
Grammar	477.29	0.0	12.04	0.0000
Vocabulary	533.72	0.0	8.27	0.0000
Fluency	445.00	0.0	2.95	0.0195
Comprehension	481.34	0.0	14.44	0.0000

Univariate degrees of freedom are 4 and 918.
Multivariate degrees of freedom are 4 and 914.

In spite of these high levels of significance, no combination of factor scores was adequate to predict completely the global proficiency ratings assigned. Table 2 shows the number of correct and incorrect predictions made by the discriminant equations. Although there was obviously a relationship between the factor scores assigned and the global proficiency ratings, the predicted scores were incorrect nearly one-third of the time. As Tables 3 and 4 show, this pattern did not change appreciably when the Spanish and French test cases were analyzed separately.

Table 2. Correct and incorrect predictions, all languages.

	Predicted rating				
Original Rating	1	2	3	4	5
1	105	18	0	0	0
2	84	205	70	1	0
3	1	75	262	16	0
4	0	0	9	52	12
5	0	0	0	3	10

N = 923; 68.7% were correctly predicted.

Table 3. Analysis of Spanish test cases.

	Predicted rating				
Original rating	1	2	3	4	5
1	14	2	1	0	0
2	11	33	12	0	0
3	1	12	52	7	0
4	0	0	2	7	1
5	0	0	0	0	2

N = 157; 68.8% were correctly predicted.

Table 4. Analysis of French test cases.

Original rating	Predicted rating				
	1	2	3	4	5
1	66	8	0	0	0
2	38	100	34	0	0
3	1	18	112	3	0
4	0	0	4	11	5
5	0	0	0	0	3

N = 403; 72.5% were correctly predicted.

Discussion. There are at least two possible reasons why FSI global ratings are not totally predictable from factor scores. First of all, it is possible that not all of the relevant factors involved in oral proficiency have been included in the system. The global FSI proficiency definitions imply, for instance, sociolinguistic skill requirements which are not specifically addressed in the factor rating descriptions. Secondly, the functionally oriented global rating procedures themselves may interfere with the relationship between factor skill and general language performance.

In examining this second possibility, it is useful to consider two prevalent philosophical approaches to language test scoring. Many tests of both linguistic and communicative competence use a total or average of the test factors or part scores in determining a candidate's general language ability. This procedure might be classified as a 'compensatory' rating system, because one can compensate for a deficiency in one factor by possessing advanced skills in one or more of the other areas rated.

A less popular approach to scoring is based on a 'noncompensatory' philosophy. In a noncompensatory system, some language factors are judged essential for effective global communication, and the global proficiency ratings assigned under this system never exceed the lowest score assigned any of the essential contributing factors. The FSI oral proficiency rating standards which rate candidates' functional language performance integrate both of these testing philosophies. Experienced testers agree that there are numerous combinations of varying factor skill levels which would qualify test candidates for a Level 1, or 'survival' level, proficiency rating. On the other hand, the functional requirement of Level 4, that the candidate 'use the language fluently and accurately', implies that minimum acceptable levels of fluency and accuracy must be met to qualify for that rating.

These examples are indicative of the criteria underlying the FSI rating scale. As one progresses along the zero-to-five proficiency scale there is a rapid increase in the complexity of the language functions described and a corresponding expansion of the noncompensatory language features required at each successive level. This relationship between language task difficulty and the complexity of the minimum essential language skills needed to perform the task is a practical, real-life phenomenon which is merely mirrored in the FSI proficiency definitions. As a result, the rating criteria are quite compensatory at the lower end of the proficiency scale, but become increasingly noncompensatory as the functional tasks become increasingly involved. At the top of the scale it could even be argued that the standards are totally noncompensatory. A test candidate, for instance, who is deficient in one or more of the factor skills would not be considered to be 'an educated native' of the language.

Conclusions. A discriminant analysis of FSI global and factor scores has revealed that although there is a significant relationship between factor skill levels and global language ability, overall proficiency ratings are not entirely predictable on the basis of factor score ratings. It is hypothesized that this inability to compute global scores mathematically from part scores may have at least two causes: (1) not all of the individual factors contributing to general language proficiency may have been identified, and (2) the functionally oriented FSI rating system appears to mix both compensatory and noncompensatory scoring criteria. Either of these conditions would preclude the development of adequate prediction equations relating factor scores to global proficiency ratings, and further research should be conducted both on the adequacy of the language factor model and on the compensatory versus noncompensatory nature of functionally oriented oral proficiency rating systems. It has been amply demonstrated that the FSI system works; continued research in these areas should yield information on why it works.

DEVELOPING AN INDIRECT MEASURE
OF OVERALL ORAL PROFICIENCY

Pardee Lowe, Jr. and Ray T. Clifford
Language School,
Central Intelligence Agency

0. Introduction. This paper discusses the goal, history, and design of the Recorded Oral Proficiency Examination (ROPE), an indirect measure of overall oral proficiency. Correlation statistics between ROPE and the CIA Language School's direct measure of overall proficiency--a version of the Foreign Service Institute oral interview--are cited, and conclusions on ROPE's accuracy, content validity, and utility are drawn. In conclusion, further research questions on ROPE and oral interview testing are posed.

0.1 Goal. The goal was to develop a 30-minute test which can be administered anywhere in the world by untrained personnel and which yields reliable, valid, and equivalent results when compared to a face-to-face oral interview on the FSI scale.

0.2 History. Originally developed for use in the International Test Validation Study of the Teachers of English to Speakers of Other Languages (TESOL) organization, ROPE was modified for use in the TESOL study because it failed to distinguish itself sufficiently in method from the other test used, the FSI oral interview. However, precisely the characteristics which spoke against ROPE's inclusion in its original form in the TESOL study spoke for its use in its original form at the CIA Language School.

1. ROPE's design. The FSI oral interview is the basic test of speaking ability used at the CIA Language School. The interview consists of a face-to-face exchange in the target language in which the candidate is asked to use the target language while talking to two native language testers. The test normally lasts 10 to 30 minutes and is recorded for verification afterwards. (See Jones 1975, Wilds 1975, Clark 1972, Lowe 1976a, for discussions on the nature of oral interview procedures.)

Increased importance has been placed on testing as the Language School's parent agency recently instituted a Language Incentive Awards program, according to which monies would be awarded to those who could prove that they speak a given language at FSI Level 3 or higher. Yet there are obviously situations in which it is impossible to administer an oral interview: where the candidate is not in the same place as the testers and where phone lines are unavailable, for example. Thus, the Language School was given the task of developing an alternative oral proficiency test which could be rated in terms of the FSI scale.

1.1 **Table of specifications.** Table 1 outlines specifications and corresponding design features. The constraints identified in this design phase have been divided in Table 1 into two general categories. In reality, the administrative and validity restrictions noted are sometimes quite interrelated and were often addressed simultaneously. In general, what was needed was a test which could be administered by anyone, which would parallel an interview, elicit about 15 minutes of natural speech from the examinee within a 30-minute period, and would be ratable using standard FSI rating criteria. In short, we hoped to achieve content validity by maintaining parallelism in structure, progression, and content. The solution was to design a prerecorded test using carefully selected questioning techniques, which also tapped the content areas usually addressed in the interview.

1.2 **Question types.** Following the requirement for maximum parallelism with the oral interview, it was decided that the recorded test would use the same kinds of questions as used in the oral interview. It was understood, of course, that one crucial element of the oral interview would be lacking: since the test would not be administered live, no follow-up of a topic or grammatical point, or change of style level or register within a given topic, would be possible. This fact clearly placed added weight on test design as the initial stimuli would have to suffice to elicit a ratable speech sample.

Parallelism was made easier because of continuing studies into the nature and effectiveness of oral interview stimuli. Lowe (1976b) contains perhaps the best overall description and specifically states the results of investigations into the levels at which a given question type is most effective. (For the FSI interview format, see Wilds in Adams and Frith 1979:39.)

Lowe distinguishes 14 question types (including two subtypes), most of them usable for both fact and opinion questions.

Table 1.

Specifications for ROPE	Resultant design features
Administrative constraints:	
Administrable by untrained personnel away from Language School	Prerecorded test
Candidates: chiefly American speakers of foreign languages	Instructions in English
No special equipment necessary	Two recorders needed: one to play ROPE cassette, another to record answers
Time: about 30 minutes overall, 15 minutes for candidate's answers	Time to answer: 15-120 seconds per question, depending on section
Validity constraints:	
Not easily compromised	Producible in equivalent forms
Sample ratable on FSI scale	Question-and-answer or task-oriented format
Sufficient quantity for ratable sample	Elicit about 15 minutes of candidate speech
Elicit natural language responses	Recorded questions in target language as stimulus
Parallel oral interview in design and progression of questions	Follow LS oral interview's four phases: warm-up, level check, and probes (wind-up on ROPE impossible, but not deemed essential in impersonal situation)
Cover whole FSI speaking range: 0+-5, while concentrating on levels of maximum interest: 2+/3	Number of questions: 20, spread over 4 sections
All levels probed using wide range of topics	Probes strengthened by requirement to continue speaking until told to stop
Primarily a speaking test; questions repeated at highest levels and time given to organize thoughts	In last two sections with mid and high level questions: 30 seconds to think about each question before answering, then question repeated before pause for answer

Type 1: Yes/No Questions. 'Do you live in Washington?'
Type 1-A: Regular Statements with Question Intonation. 'You went to the museum?'
Type 2: Alternative Answer Questions. 'How did you get to work this morning--by bus, or by car?'
Type 3: Polite Requests. 'Please pass me the ashtray.'
Type 4: Information Questions. 'Who was with you?'
Type 4-A: Information Questions with Props (for example, questions about pictures or objects in the testing room).
Type 5: S-1 Situations. In a simulation, candidate is asked, for example, to arrange for an inexpensive hotel room.
Type 6: Candidate-Interviews-Testers. Candidate is instructed to seek information from testers.
Type 7: Rephrasable Questions. 'Please explain the law-making functions of the Congress.'/'How do the House and Senate make laws?'
Type 8: Hypothetical Questions. 'If you had known last week that you would be working in Washington, what plans would you have made?'
Type 9: Unknown Situations. 'You're the manager of a small office with two secretaries and a *receptionist*. Your old receptionist leaves. Explain to an employment agency your requirements for a *replacement: neatly dressed, outgoing*, must answer phone in a *friendly voice*.'
Type 10: Descriptive Preludes. 'Some people feel that a college education should lead directly to employment; others hold that it should train the mind in general. What is your view?'
Type 11: Conversational Prelude. A variation of the descriptive prelude in which two testers express opposing points of view and ask the examinee for his opinion.
Type 12: Candidate Prompted Questions. A question which arises from a personal or professional interest of the examinee: 'How do the German and American school systems compare in your experience?'

Not all types lend themselves readily to a recorded test. For example, Yes/No Questions, without follow-up, produce too little information to be useful. Others, such as Regular Statements with Question Intonation, are unsuited to non-face-to-face testing situations. Still others, such as Rephrasable Questions, depend on the nature and course of the candidate's answer--another area in which a single recorded stimulus is insufficient. Since ROPE was designed to be self-sufficient, Information Questions with Props are also out of the question, as are Candidate Prompted Questions. Thus, five question types (Yes/No, Regular Statements with Question Intonation, Alternative Answer Questions, Rephrasable Questions, and Candidate Prompted Questions) were immediately eliminated from consideration.

The Candidate-Interviews-Testers type was considered unsuitable for the first version of the test but by careful structuring could conceivably be adopted in later ROPEs.

S-1 Situations and Unknown Situations were considered problematical for the first ROPE version. It is conceivable that they could be adapted in later ROPEs, particularly if probes can be adequately built in so as to gain the maximum amount of specific information about the candidate's level in the minimum amount of time.

Obviously, Candidate Prompted Questions (topics which the candidate brings up) are excluded from ROPE, primarily because the chance of a memorized atypical sample is too great and could, without probing by actual testers, bias the raters' evaluation of the sample.

For ease of recording, Conversational Prelude was left untried in ROPE, since at least two different voices are required.

The foregoing considerations eliminated 10 of the 14 question types from ROPE use. The remaining four types were used in ROPE to varying degrees. Table 2 contains the types and the levels at which each type (without considering specific topical content) is generally most useful (for more detail see Lowe 1976b).

Table 2.

Question type	Range of levels	Optimal level
Information Questions	0+ - 5	0+ - 3
Polite Requests	0 - 4+	0+ - 4+
Hypothetical Questions	1+/2* - 5	3 - 4+
Descriptive Prelude Questions	2+/3 - 5	3 - 5

*Starting level depends on the relative difficulty of this construction in any specific language, although topically it is most useful at 2+/3 level and above.

The utility of Information Questions can be shifted to the 2+/3 level and above, if the topical content demands supported opinion. The first version of ROPE contains 10 Information Questions, 4 Polite Requests, 2 Hypothetical Questions, and 4 Descriptive Prelude Questions. Of these, 8 are Opinion Questions.

1.3 Distribution of question types. In FSI interviews, one observes a progression of subject matter, starting with social amenities and survival topics at the lowest level and progressing through personal common concrete subjects to opinions, abstract concepts, and problem solving. Some question types are more appropriate than others for each topic and to each level to the extent that topics correspond to levels on the FSI scale. It must be understood that the question only indicates a possible range of response levels; the examinee's usage

determines the actual level of his response. (For fuller
description of the FSI levels, see Adams and Frith 1979 for
'Definitions of absolute ratings' and Lowe 1976a:7, 'LLC guidelines for assigning language proficiency levels', which supplements the basic FSI Definitions.) Table 3 gives a graphic
representation of the levels covered by each question in the
first English version ROPE. It may be noted that all levels
are sampled more than once and that questions fall on both
sides of the important 2+/3 border.

Table 3. Distribution of ROPE questions across FSI levels.

English Version 1

Section	Question number	0+	1	1+	2	2+	3	3+	4	4+	5
Section 1	1		——	——							
	2	——	——	——							
	3		——	——							
	4		——	——							
Section 2	5	——	——	——							
	6				——	——					
	7			——	——	——					
	8	——	——	——	——	——					
	9			——	——						
	10					——	——	——			
	11		——	——	——						
Section 3	12				——	——	——	——	——	——	——
	13				——	——	——	——	——	——	
	14				——	——	——	——	——	——	
	15					——	——	——	——	——	
	16						——	——			
	17							——	——	——	
Section 4	18				——	——	——	——	——	——	——
	19				——	——	——	——	——	——	——
	20								——	——	——

The following are samples of the various questions used in
the first ROPE.

Part 1:   1 'What's the weather like today?' (S-1)
          (Information Question)

Part 2:   5 'Describe what you are wearing.' (S-0+/1)
          (Polite Request)

          10 'If you were granted your fondest wish, what
          would you do and why?' (S-2+/3)

Part 3: 14 'What is the goal of a college education? Some
hold that it should lead directly to employment,
others that it should train the mind in general.
What is your view?' (S-2/5)
(Descriptive Prelude Question)

1.4 **Modifications.** Shortly after ROPE was designed and
field tested, it became evident that two modifications should
be undertaken in future versions.

First, because of the problem of test compromise, further
versions should be recorded using different questions, rather
than the now monolithic version which appears in language
after language with the same topics and questions. The first
version is, with some cultural modification, a truly parallel
set of tests in the several languages in which ROPE exists.

Second, initial concern that too much time had been allo-
cated for the candidate's answer proved unfounded. In fact,
the reverse was true and it now appears that future ROPEs
should have the time for answers lengthened. Raters felt
that the length of the speech sample was adequate, but test
candidates repeatedly expressed the opinion that they needed
more time to discuss the topics presented.

2. **The correlation study.** Since the ROPE was specifically
designed to parallel the oral interview and to provide information equivalent to that obtained from the standard procedure, it was important to know how well the results of these
two assessment procedures correlated.

To date, a total of 27 ROPEs have been administered to
candidates who have also been tested by oral interview in
French, German, and Spanish. This number represents the
total of those subjects who met two criteria: an oral interview test had been administered during the previous three
months, and the candidate was currently available for retest-
ing. Nine German, 11 French, and 7 Spanish subjects, with
skills ranging from Level 0+ to Level 5, met these requirements. These subjects were given the recorded examination
and then ratings were assigned using standard rating procedures and rating criteria. Table 4 summarizes the results of
this pilot study.

Table 4. Statistical comparison of interview and ROPE
ratings (n = 27; r = .90).

Test	Mean	S.D.
Interview	2.67	1.21
ROPE	2.45	1.24

Results and recommendations. The results of the interview and ROPE testing were quite comparable. The slightly lower mean score for the ROPE procedure is not statistically significant and may simply be the result of scoring recorded (rather than live-language) samples. The correlation of .90 between testing methods was especially encouraging, considering the substantial length of time which had often elapsed between the interview and subsequent ROPE administration. Although this correlation provided substantial evidence of concurrent validity for the alternate ROPE procedure, the primary concern of personnel managers was the 'decision validity' of ROPE ratings. That is, would using ROPE ratings produce the same managerial decisions as using FSI oral interview ratings?

Since 'professional proficiency', Level 3, is the critical score for most managerial decisions, it was selected as the determinant score in constructing the agreement matrix displayed in Table 5.

Table 5. Selection validity for Level 3 and higher.

Subjects as rated by interview	Subjects as rated by ROPE		
	Below Level 3	Level 3 and above	Total
Below Level 3	18	1	19
Level 3 and above	1	7	8
Total	19	8	27

Using Level 3 as the selection criterion resulted in agreement between the interview and recorded testing procedures on 25 of the 27 subjects. The other two cases showed no pattern of disagreement, with each method being more conservative on one of the two cases. While these results are definitely positive, they must be interpreted with caution until more data become available. Despite the small size of the pilot project, however, it does appear that alternate test elicitation procedures can be developed which have satisfactory validity to be used where conditions preclude true interview testing. The Recorded Oral Proficiency Exam is clearly a step in that direction.

REFERENCES

Adams, Marianne Lehr, and James R. Frith, eds. 1979. Testing kit: French and Spanish. Washington, D.C.: U.S. Department of State.

Clark, John L. D. 1972. FSI language proficiency interview. In: Foreign language testing: Theory and practice. Philadelphia: Center for Curriculum Development. 121-129.

Clark, John L. D., ed. 1978. Direct testing of speaking proficiency: Theory and application. Princeton, N.J.: Educational Testing Service.

Clifford, Ray T. 1977. Reliability and validity of language
aspects contributing to oral proficiency of prospective teach-
ers of German. In: Clark, ed. (1978:191-209).
Jones, Randall L. 1975. Testing speaking proficiency. In:
Jones and Spolsky, eds. (1975:1-7).
Jones, Randall L., and Bernard Spolsky, eds. 1975. Testing
language proficiency. Arlington, Va.: Center for Applied
Linguistics.
Lowe, Pardee, Jr. 1976a. The oral language proficiency test.
Washington, D.C.: U.S. Government Interagency Language
Roundtable. 1-15.
Lowe, Pardee, Jr. 1976b. Handbook on question types and
their use in LS oral proficiency tests. Washington, D.C.:
CIA Language School.
Wilds, Claudia P. 1975. The oral interview test. In: Jones
and Spolsky, eds. (1975:29-38).

EVALUATING SECOND LANGUAGE ORAL PROFICIENCY IN THE CANADIAN GOVERNMENT

Roger E. Mareschal
Public Service Commission of Canada,
Language Services Directorate

There are two major areas of evaluation activity in the language field within the Canadian government. One is related to legal requirements, i.e. evaluating incumbents of, or candidates for, bilingual positions; the other is pedagogical, i.e. evaluating individuals during or at the end of language training. The first is a responsibility of the Staffing Branch of the Public Service Commission; the second is a responsibility of the Language Training Branch of the Public Service Commission.

Common preoccupations among the various agencies involved in the language domain are training and testing in relationship with 'the capacity to do the job'. In order to operationalize this preoccupation and to translate it into pragmatic activities, we believe that some analysis must be conducted before people are sent to training, especially since training may take up to 12 months.

The first step we go through is to analyze the institutional needs in the language field. In our situation where private citizens as well as public servants have, by law, certain rights as to the services they can request in either of the official languages (English or French), we want to make sure not only that the services are rendered (effectiveness) but also that the services are rendered economically (efficiency). Thus, from an institutional point of view, once a firm need has been identified and translated into an objective, one has to consider the means to be used, among which training an individual is but one of the possible solutions to attain the objective.

Other possibilities include the use of bilingual documentation, parallel unilingual positions, and remote audio-video communication (when the need for the other official language does not justify the full-time presence of a bilingual capacity). Considering the expense--both financial and human--involved when sending somebody to training, we think that these alternate possibilities have to be looked at from an institutional point of view before decisions are made. Indeed, when managers send (lose) somebody to training for up to 12 months, they want to be able to relate their decision to the situation they are in, the actual needs identified, the need to have incumbents in the positions to do the work that has to be done.

Sending somebody to training must be inserted within a logical framework where a sequenced institutional analysis of *situation → needs → objectives → means* has been carried out. Training is just one of the *means* from the organizational point of view.

Before we reach the level of the individual we need an intermediary tool which consists in the definition mode of the results expected in order to attain the institution's needs through the individual's competency. One preliminary remark: we should not equate needs and objectives; often only a few of the needs can reasonably be met because of constraints in time, budget, or other resources. This should be made clear at all stages to avoid false perceptions or expectations among any of the players in this intricate game.

Depending on the definition mode chosen, the institution may end up with rather differing results. The basis for description can vary all the way from grammatical and linguistic elements (what language is) to functional/notional elements (what one does with language), with the implications one can expect from these differing approaches. In one instance, expectations will tend to be heavy on the knowledge end; in the other, they will be shifted to the capacity to carry out the actions that are expected. In the first case, what will be evaluated is, for instance, the knowledge of the future tense; in the second, it will be the capacity to brief (which does require the use of the future tense). Thus an early decision is required to direct the work of curriculum specialists, material and test developers, students, and teachers. Do we specify what learners need to *do* with language or do we specify what learners need to *know*, leaving the determination of the content to the specialists? Since in our situation in the Canadian Public Service Commission we are aiming at a certification of capacity to do a job, we are led to focus on 'linguistic intent' rather than on 'linguistic content'.

Thus when, at the individual level, we do the *situation → needs → objectives → means → evaluation* analysis, we bear this bias in mind all along, including at the evaluation level.

When working in pedagogy, the evaluation tools must be in keeping with the approach used in the needs analysis and in the development of teaching materials. As we see in the examples further on in this paper, we have to find means to evaluate the capacity to perform in a second language according to the description of what the person is supposed to do in the job. Intent is what matters. Content is only a secondary means to operationalize the intent. Content will, of course, always be present but in most cases, once we are beyond the elementary level, the strategy used to operationalize the intent is not the main element to be considered unless it is an integral part of the description of the objective being pursued.

It must be added that we are in a situation where professional competence in the first official language is taken as a given before training commences and is not taken into account as a variable to be measured or as a constraint--although in some instances this competence has been known to be inadequate.

When considering content, we look not only at language in terms of forms or in terms of a code but also in terms of a means to attain an intent which is both pragmatically functional and sociolinguistically appropriate. We need to work in the area of awareness of possible strategies used by the speaker to attain a given result in different situations with different relationships between the speakers. It is also necessary to ensure that we maintain coherence in the format used for evaluation. If language only occurs when there is an intent-- when a concrete result is expected--we should deliberately stay away from approaches which--by requiring mechanistic or decontextualized use of the language--would bias the results.

All testing strategies consequently have to be in a 'meaningful' context; we know that 'real' contexts are illusory in a pedagogical setting but we can certainly maintain a constant 'realistic' setting. If one wants to test grammar, one can easily select situations where certain grammatical events necessarily occur, e.g. reporting for past tense, briefing for future tense. Typologies can be established which will enable item writers to be able to use realistic settings whenever they want to test an element of the linguistic code. This approach can be used within an 'objective', 'discrete point' type test. This type of format does not prevent a situational approach.

In fact, we realize that when we speak about a functional approach we have to look at two types of functionalism: first, the functional relationship between the language and the job (institutional level); second, the functional relationship between the linguistic tasks and the linguistic content (individual level).

It becomes evident from the preceding that a functional approach must incorporate the parameters of sociolinguistics. Functionalism as regards pedagogical activities also means keeping to essentials, that is, learning what is necessary to enable the individual who is confronted with an intent to be translated into an utterance to find the solution as quickly as possible with minimal effort. A functional approach, as developed through adult education, deals with precise needs within a limited time frame and requires a different student and teacher

involvement. The first concern, as we have seen, is to rede-
fine the learning (testing) object as language basically becomes
a means of performing intentions. Language performance means
mastering adequate speech acts in which discourse coherence
overrides sentence cohesion. Communicative competence is
attained not so much by the intrinsic meaning of the utterances
as by their useful value in the context in which they take
place.

The concepts of the functional approach, with regard to
either the process or the language, explain why our project with the security officers of National Museums for instance is more than a mere list of specialized vocabulary.
The vocabulary lists constituting specialized types of
French will always remain formal and static taxonomies,
whereas the speech acts of the functional approach define
a dynamic and useful object. This is also why the project
did not simply adapt existing methods or materials. To
paraphrase Louis Porcher, we are not changing very much
by substituting 'This is a Rembrandt painting' for 'This
is Mr. Thibaut'. There is no guarantee that the language
needs of a given clientele will be met by adapting situational elements of a structural method to the clientele--ele-
ments that are really only a pretext, a way of presenting
morphosyntactic elements with no specific context. The
functional approach therefore requires a renewed approach
to the conception and development of teaching materials for
classroom use as well as for purposes of assessment.[1]

It is indispensable, when developing and implementing pedagogical tools (curriculum, teaching materials, evaluation tools),
that specialists work in close coordination with students,
supervisors (they are the ones who really know why they
send their people to language training), teachers, and test
developers.

Tests used in an administrative setting.[2] Within the
Canadian public service, language proficiency is presently
measured in four abilities with a three-level scale for each.
In the context of this paper, I will focus on the oral proficiency subtest used for the highest level, labeled 'C' in our
system.

This oral proficiency subtest, which we developed in 1975
and have been using since 1976, consists in a four-part interview designed to elicit a sample of general language performance from each candidate. We have to bear in mind that we
are in a situation where jobs are at stake and that we had to
devise a system which would ensure both high face validity
and ease of scoring. Be it noted that we not only wanted
identical scores from different scorers but that we wanted
identical scores for identical reasons!

Research from other institutions (ETS, CIA, FSI, DLI, ARELS) as well as our own findings indicated that a relatively short sample representative of a candidate's oral communication was sufficient to derive a valid score. On that basis, but with a serious constraint at the face-validity level and assuming that real language performance can vary (depending on such factors as the situation, the subject, and the degree of stress), it was decided to design a four-part interview of approximately 30 minutes to obtain samples from which to derive reliable estimates of general performance level.

The proposed communication situations were selected on the basis of their probable formality and probable familiarity to the candidates in order to cover adequately a variety of situations (personal experience, personal interests, work-related matters, subjects of general interest).

It was postulated that these four areas would cover the kinds of situations most typical of language use among the candidates: formal and informal language, well integrated and more general vocabulary. An interviewer conducts the interview while an observer ensures that a sufficient sample is obtained and that no memorization is involved in the candidate's performance.

Our point of view was that three major components constitute meaningful indicators of communicative competence: (1) the 'linguistic code elements' used (grammatical, vocabulary, phonological); (2) the relative availability of these means in a speaking situation (adequate realization of a communicative intent with the proper content within a limited time frame); and (3) the accuracy with which the speaker uses the code to emit more or less adequate utterances in a given situation.

In terms of functional communicative competence, the last two components (fluency and accuracy) are fundamental to the effectiveness and efficiency a speaker can demonstrate in a language performance situation. If fluency is lacking, the listener is likely to drift off or to switch to the first language of the speaker; if, on the other hand, accuracy is too low, the message becomes incomprehensible and results in a breach of communication. A balance must be maintained between these two components with the support of adequate code elements.

When we looked for an adequate means of evaluating oral performance, most scales in use put little emphasis on fluency and accuracy components but were heavy on code elements (grammar, vocabulary, pronunciation, etc.) using the 'educated native speaker' as a model. We did not consider these approaches suitable for our purpose, nor did we feel we could incorporate level of abstraction, variety of strategies, etc., in our evaluation of a general level of second language proficiency unrelated to education or IQ.

We found the system developed by Nicholas Ferguson at the Centre Experimental pour l'Enseignement des Langues (CEEL) in Geneva[3] to be more appropriate to our aims. This system, based on Shannon's mathematical theory of communication and on the stochastic process, retained two variables in order to determine a score of second language oral proficiency: fluency and syntactic correctness. The final score is a function of the two variables taken together. In his system Ferguson uses tone groups as a basis for scoring fluency (number of tone groups per minute) and correctness: 'A tone group is composed of one stress group with primary stress together with other less prominent stress groups round it. It gives a basic unit of information'.[4] He provided experimental evidence that fluency and accuracy are the most significant factors to be used in evaluating general second language oral proficiency. Here is an example from Ferguson (// = tone group, / = stress group):

// The children/get up/at 8 o'clock//and their mother/prepares breakfast/for the family//. Their father/goes to work/after breakfast//while the children/go to school//.[4]

Following the stochastic model, we can say that the production of a simple correct word of English or French is a first order approximation to English or French, the production of a stress group (linking two or more words) is a second order approximation to English or French, the production of a tone group (linking two or more stress groups) is a third order approximation to English or French. The more complex the order of approximation mastered by a speaker, the higher the mastery of a language, e.g. *Father* vs. *Father goes to* vs. *Father goes to the movies.*

Conversely, the simpler the order of approximation not mastered by a speaker, the lower the mastery of a language, as in the following example.

'Me go' (instead of 'I'), 'I go in' (instead of 'to'),
  (S_1) (S_2)

'I go to the movies yesterday.'
  (S_3) (instead of 'went')

In the scoring system, errors at S_1 level are given the most weight (0 correctness), errors at S_2 level are given .25 value, S_3 errors are given the least weight and earn .5 value, and error-free tone groups get 1. The score is then calculated by computing fluency in tone group per minute:

$$\left(\frac{\Sigma \text{ tone groups}}{\Sigma \text{ time (in minutes)}} \right)$$

and by adding up the value of each tone group scored for correctness as indicated above to obtain ΣC:

$$w\,T_1 \times \quad 0 = 0$$
$$x\,T_2 \times \quad .25 = a$$
$$y\,T_3 \times \quad .50 = b$$
$$z\,T_c \times 1.00 = \underline{c}$$

$$\boxed{\Sigma C} = \frac{a + b + C}{x + y + z}$$

The final score is a standardized mathematical function of these two scores illustrated in a standard score table (cf. Appendix 1), with correctness on the vertical axis and fluency on the horizontal axis.

In Ferguson's system, relatively equal weight is given to fluency and correctness in the range of standardized scores we find near our pass score. Candidates can nevertheless compensate to a certain extent for low fluency by high correctness and vice versa.

In Ferguson's standardization of the relationship between the two factors, it was found that for incorrect candidates relatively smaller increases in fluency would have significant impact on a candidate's ranking. For very correct candidates, however, there is relatively little variation with fluency and variation is not significant relative to the score required to pass. Thus, even very slow first language speakers have no problem in passing the test because all score high on the accuracy factor.

For extremely fluent candidates, small increases in accuracy cause significant increases in score above a minimum accuracy threshold while for extremely slow candidates, increases in accuracy are practically meaningless below a certain threshold.

When the interviews are scored, stretches of discourse are selected that best represent the normal capacity of the examinee. The scorer is expected to score as if he were a real listener who tries to derive a global understanding of what is said. If an error is missed, a normal listener does not normally backtrack, nor should a scorer do so.

Of course, the smoother the discourse, the better the chance that it will be perceived as correct. As the scorer's decisions cumulate, the candidate's score tends to stabilize. Each decision of the scorer can be viewed as a score on an item on an objective test. Each candidate's final score is based on 80 to 140 decisions to ensure stability and reliability to scores obtained on the basis of four samples of approximately two minutes each. The guidelines given to the candidate can be found in Appendix 2.

Tests used in a pedagogical setting. The Language Training Branch has completely revised its French curriculum in the last two years and has made the necessary alterations to gear it in the direction of a fundamentally functional-notional-andragogical approach. Consequently, a mandate was given to our Evaluation Service to develop an integrated system for evaluating student performance, taking into account these new orientations. Since the evaluation system is an integral and continuous part of the student's language acquisition experience, it begins with preliminary orientation and continues throughout the system. We have stressed the 'system' aspect because we wanted evaluation to be coherent both in relationship to the new curriculum as a whole and in the relationship of each of its components to the others. The evaluation system thus undertakes to measure student progress in terms of both linguistic and communicative abilities. The new curriculum is composed of three major parts: cycle 1 and cycle 2 in sequence plus language of work modules which can be used at any time during either cycle. The evaluation system proposes three types of measurement instruments: 'required', 'complementary', and 'supplementary' for each one of these parts. The required type must be administered and results must be entered in cumulative file; the complementary is highly recommended as an indicator of progress; and the supplementary is used optionally as required by students or teachers. The objective and use of each instrument is clearly indicated to both instructors and students so as to guide them in the selection and use of these instruments. I will focus here on the oral communication evaluation grids which may be of interest to persons involved in evaluation within training activities.

Appendix 3 reproduces the oral communication evaluation grid for the lower level. The grids for the two other levels are identical in design except for the fact that criterion 1 (conveys message) decreases from a value of 30 at the first level to 25 at the second level and 10 at the third level; conversely, criterion 2 (communication components) increases from 20 at the first level to 25 at the second level and 40 at the third level. These changes in weight from one level to the other allow for global capacity to be the central focus at the outset of training, with a gradual transfer of weight to accuracy at later stages of language acquisition.

Oral communication is thus divided into two parts: conveying the message and communication components. The former includes the student's ability to convey a message by producing utterances which are appropriate to the communication situation, whilst the latter allows for the evaluation of content used in the communication process, including the sociolinguistic dimension proper to the situation: functions, subfunctions, status, attitudes, locale, theme, etc.

In order to ensure minimal uniformity, scorers are provided with definition tables for each category of elements taken into account when attributing a mark (see samples in Appendices 4 and 5a,b).

Another type of oral proficiency evaluation is provided by the new 'Group oral communication tests'[5] developed by our Evaluation Service. This evaluation tool tries to do away with the constraints usually imposed on both developers and

students. Major constraints for the test developer are to:
(1) find tricks to make artificial situations look more natural
and conducive to spontaneous speech; (2) entice confidence on
the part of the student; (3) develop a tool which is simple,
easy to score, short, and valid. Major constraints for the student are to: (1) speak in a contrived setting; (2) speak to a
machine or react to artificial questions which are posed for the
sake of evaluation only; (3) stay within the strict limits of the
question; (4) remember all the components of the question; (5)
elaborate on an artificial stimulus.

The aims of the group communication tests are thus: (1) to
evaluate the capacity of the students to transmit a verbal message in the second language which will be understandable to a
native listener (scores: 2, 1, or 0); (2) to evaluate the ease
with which the information is provided (fluency) (scores: 1 or
0); (3) to evaluate the quality of the utterances in terms of
pronunciation (scores: 1 or 0).

The very format chosen and technique used will also do away
with a few stressing factors inasmuch as (1) the subject is
chosen by the group of students amongst a list of possible
subjects; (2) the conversation takes place amongst students in
a spontaneous mode; and (3) any classroom is suitable (no need
for language lab).

Our experimentation to date shows that 15 ideas (one or two
sentences per idea) per student allow for a reliable evaluation
without undue limitation of the conversation. A bonus can be
given to those students who produce over 15 utterances (up to
10 marks). The score is thus established as follows:

Message	(2, 1, or 0)	× 15	30 max
Fluency	(1 or 0)	× 15	15 max
Pronunciation	(1 or 0)	× 15	15 max
Supplementary	(1 or 0)	× 10	10 max
utterances			70 max
(bonus)			

Since the evaluation is made at the global level of ideas expressed through sentences (with or without grammatical mistakes; ideas expressed without mistakes, being more readily
understood, get the higher score of 2), it becomes easy to
score at the message level as the conversation occurs, provided the instructor does not allow two persons to speak at
the same time. Since pronunciation and fluency are on a 1
(good) or 0 (hesitates) scale, this part of the scoring can be
carried out at the same time.

The foregoing approach has been validated. The data
gathered to date on oral expression yielded a Spearman correlation of .727 when correlated with the independent overall
ratings given by seven teachers on a seven-point scale to 140
subjects. When the sums of the oral comprehension and oral
expression scores were correlated with the teachers'

independent ratings using the Spearman formula, the correlation was .754. The average inter-scorer reliability for pairs of raters when calculated for the same sample was .835.

We are thus led to believe that this approach is not only simple and fast but also reliable. We are convinced that it will allow us to improve considerably on the information provided to teachers and students in the acquisition process without undue technical interruptions usually required by evaluation procedures.

In the field of more specific oral proficiency tests I again draw from the security officers project we conducted for the National Museum to illustrate a possible approach in this area. The very outline of the interview situation used for this evaluation indicates how one can apply a job-specific functional approach at the evaluation stage.

(1) *Aim of the interview.* The interview, which in effect is an achievement test, aims at measuring the attainment of the objectives of the specific training programme developed for the security officers. Both the training programme and the interview-test are directly aimed at the language needs related to the functions and tasks of these officers.

(2) *Design of the interview.* The interview is designed to last approximately 35 minutes and includes 57 items grouped in three parts.

Part 1 (30 items) aims at measuring the capacity to carry out tasks in French related to the functions of 'Surveillance' and 'Emergency'. In real-life situations the types of language behaviour expected in such cases are in direct relationship with events perceived by means of visual stimuli. In this first part students are given indications in English as to what is happening which requires their oral intervention.

Example: Two young children are running in one of the sections of the museum while their mother is looking at an exhibit. Speak to them.

Parts 2 (17 items) and 3 (10 items) aim at measuring the capacity to carry out tasks in French related to the functions of 'Information giving' and 'Commenting'. These tasks require the capacity to understand French messages and the capacity to answer in the appropriate manner. Role-playing activities were selected to evaluate these capacities. At the beginning of these two parts candidates must be assigned working posts according to actual assignments. (The various possibilities are indicated in the interview guide.) This approach allows for verifying the accuracy of information given. For example (translated):

Could you tell me where I can find
(a) the souvenir shop (National Gallery),
(b) the gift shop (Science and Technology Museum),
(c) the First World War section (War Museum),
(d) the Lancaster aircraft (Air Museum)?

In part 3, some items involve the capacity to translate into English messages of an urgent nature. For example:

French stimulus: 'There is a lost handbag in room no. 4.'
Tell me what this person just said.

(3) *Scoring procedures*. Four factors are judged in scoring each utterance following a question: 'comprehensibility', 'content', 'appropriateness', and 'organization'. These factors are evaluated in a precise step-by-step decision-making sequence. The items of the interview cover such tasks as 'offer', 'warn', 'explain', 'threaten', 'accept', and 'reassure', to name a few.

Step 1. This step is designed to determine if the message is understandable or not. If, after hearing it twice, it is not comprehensible, a 0 score is attributed and no further consideration is given to the utterance. If comprehensible, the scorer proceeds to Step 2.

Step 2. Within the course objectives, 'content' is of utmost importance. It constitutes a prerequisite to be met in order to determine whether the scorer proceeds to Steps 3 and 4 or not. If the required 'content' is not obtained, the scorer does not go any further because the job-related linguistic task has in fact not been carried out. In judging 'content', the scorer must determine whether the required elements of behaviour were given by the candidate. Three types of utterances are required according to the task to be performed; to wit, language behaviour requiring one element, two elements, or three elements.

Example of a language behaviour requiring one element:

'You notice a person entering your section. He is stumbling and you fear he might fall.' ('offer')

The answer must be something like the following:

Avez-vous besoin d'aide? ('Do you need any help?')
or
Est-ce que je peux vous aider? ('Can I help you?')

Example of a language behaviour requiring two elements:

'You have told a young lady that eating or drinking is prohibited in the museum. Later on you see her walking around with a cup of coffee in her hands. She did not pay attention to your request. Speak to her.'

The answer should be something like this:

Element 1 ('warn').   Madame, je vous ai dit qu'il est
interdit de boire dans le musée ...
('Madam, I have already told you that drinking is
prohibited in the museum ...')
Element 2 ('explain').   ... Vous pouvez abîmer les articles
exposés
ou
... C'est un règlement du musée.
('... You could ruin the exhibits'
or
'... It is a museum rule').

In the case where one element is required, the scorer determines whether this condition has been filled and, if satisfied,
gives the 100 percent mark (see grid in Appendix 6).

In the case where two elements are required, success in one
element yields 50 percent, success in both, 100 percent.

In the case where three elements are required, success in at
least two elements is required and yields a score of 66 percent;
three elements give 100 percent.

If Step 2 has been successfully attained, the scorer proceeds
to Step 3, where 'appropriateness' is evaluated in terms of the
use of *tu* and *vous* and in terms of singular and plural.   In
Step 3, the score can be either 0 or 100 percent (0 or 1).   In
order to get 100 percent, the candidate should make no mistake.
A failure at this point does not interrupt the scoring.

At Step 4, the 'organization' of the discourse is evaluated in
terms of the following linguistic errors: structural errors ('I
not seen the boys'); agreement errors ('The boys is down-
stairs'); and use of slang English words, longer than normal
hesitation.   The possible marks are 0 or 1.   In order to get
the 1 mark, the utterance should not include more than two
errors.

Each item in the interview is evaluated in terms of Steps 1
to 4, and scores are added within the factors of 'content',
'appropriateness', and 'organization'.   Each factor has its own
minimal required total score (39, 45, 41, respectively).   When
a candidate succeeds at the interview, we can certify that his
capacity to perform the required tasks has been evaluated
within a functional framework which is meaningful and informative to all parties concerned.   We also are assured that this
approach allows for a much more efficient use of the time and
energy devoted to training and evaluation than is allowed by
more traditional content-oriented approaches.

By providing a clear specification grid of language functions
and tasks to be performed within a certain number of settings,
we provide every player with basic data allowing for a
criterion-referenced approach which, when one has practical
efficiency in mind, is the only one that can be adopted.

No one would consider entering into a contract which specified only that a 10-mile road was to be built. One would want
to specify from where to where, for what kind of load, with
what kind of surface, etc. In the language training field, however (and one could broaden this to most other training areas),
people tend to act without specifications. Millions of dollars
are spent to 'learn a language' with no more details given: no
purpose, no context, no indications of areas of use.

Our endeavour to be explicit on these points may look self-
detrimental when we think of the innumerable excuses we could
use if no specifications were provided which could later be used
by our clients as criteria to evaluate our success or failure.
Nevertheless, it was in full awareness of this that we decided
to go this route. We think that the whole profession will bene-
fit from such approaches and that our own activities will be
greatly facilitated through the enhanced understanding of our
work by our clients at all levels. The examples given here
are but first-stage attempts at functionalizing our field, but
they lead us to believe that it is a meaningful step forward in
providing users with more acceptable evaluation tools in oral
proficiency.

NOTES

1. Adapted from P. Naud, Report on 'Welcome to the
Museum', Language Training Program for Security Officers at
National Museums, Linguistic Services Directorate, Public Service Commission, Ottawa, 1979, 17 pp.
2. For a more detailed description refer to: R. Friedman,
500A Oral Expression Sub-Test in Medium, Pedagogical Journal,
Vol. 3, No. 3, July, 1978, p. 57 and following. Available
upon request from The Editor, Medium, Linguistic Services
Directorate, Pedagogical Resources Service, Asticou Development Centre, Cité des Jeunes Blvd., Room 1666, Hull, Québec,
Canada, K1A OM7.
3. N 73 Test, To evaluate the overall spoken language control of adult speakers of English as a foreign language.
N. Ferguson, CEEL, Geneva, 1973.
4. Oral Language Analyser and Feedback System (OLAF)
Instantaneous Measurement of Spoken Language Skills.
N. Ferguson, CEEL, Geneva, Roneo, 6 pp., 1975.
5. Jenny Svider, Test de communication verbale en groupe,
1978 (unpublished).

APPENDIX 1.

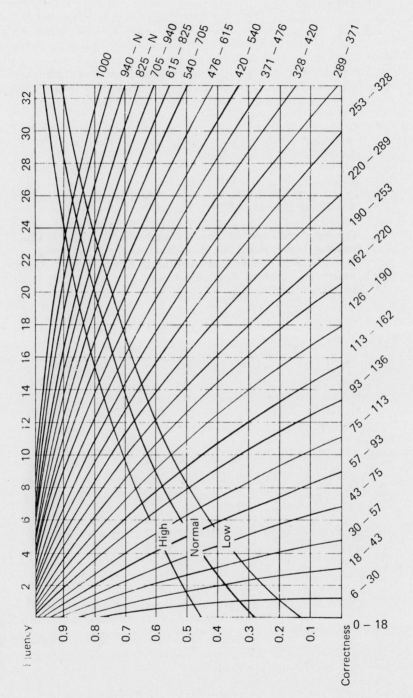

APPENDIX 2.

General Guidelines for the Oral Expression Sub-test

1. In this sub-test, you are evaluated on how fluently and accurately you use French to communicate in an interview situation and *not on the content of what you say.*

2. Since we wish to evaluate your fluency and accuracy in speaking French, you should say as much as you can on any point of discussion.

3. However, you are not expected to give a formal speech or a perfectly structured presentation of your ideas. Speak as you would in a normal conversation.

4. Except for names of people, places or certain trade names, avoid using English during the interview. If you cannot remember a particular word, try to explain what you mean in French rather than using the equivalent term in English.

APPENDIX 3.

Oral Communication Evaluation: Cycle 1 - Level A

Student:_____   Unit:_____

Administrator/corrector:_____   Teaching Unit:_____   Group:_____

CRITERIA	SITUATIONS					GRAND TOTAL
	____	____	____	____	____	
1. CONVEYS MESSAGE, OUT OF 30 TOTAL 1 =	1 2 3 4 5 x6= /30	1 2 3 4 5 x6= /30	1 2 3 4 5 x6= /30	1 2 3 4 5 x6= /30	1 2 3 4 5 x6= /30	
2. COMMUNICATION COMPONENTS, OUT OF 20						
(a) COMPREHENSION	1 2 3 4 5	1 2 3 4 5	1 2 3 4 5	1 2 3 4 5	1 2 3 4 5	
(b) SOCIOLINGUISTIC ASPECTS	1 2 3 4 5	1 2 3 4 5	1 2 3 4 5	1 2 3 4 5	1 2 3 4 5	
(c) GRAMMATICAL ASPECTS	1 2 3 4 5	1 2 3 4 5	1 2 3 4 5	1 2 3 4 5	1 2 3 4 5	
(d) FLUENCY	1 2 3 4 5	1 2 3 4 5	1 2 3 4 5	1 2 3 4 5	1 2 3 4 5	
TOTAL 2 =	/20	/20	/20	/20	/20	↓
Total: (1 + 2) x 2	/100	/100	/100	/100	/100	

FINAL RESULT
AS A PERCENTAGE: GRAND TOTAL_____ ÷ NUMBER OF SITUATIONS_____ = | /100 |

AREAS REQUIRING ATTENTION

SOCIOLINGUISTIC:_____
_____
_____

GRAMMATICAL:_____
_____
_____

FLUENCY:_____
_____
_____

STRATEGY:_____
_____
_____

APPENDIX 4.

Tableau des Composantes. Situation B.

| Fonctions | Sous-fonctions | Parametres | | Agents: | Situation |
		Thème	Canal	étudiant/examinateur	
obtenir action	demander à parler à quelqu'un (15)	responsable de la climatisation	au téléphone	étudiant/adjoint	au bureau
	commenter (19)	la température au bureau			
	transmettre un message (15)	au sujet de la température			
	commenter (9)	la situation		étudiant/responsable	

Table of Components. Situation B.

| Functions | Sub-functions | Parameters | | Agents: | Situation |
		Theme	Channel	student/examiner	
to obtain action	to ask for somebody	person in charge of air conditioning	over the phone	student/agent	in the office
	to comment	office temperature			
	to transmit a message	about temperature			
	to comment	the situation		student/person in charge	

APPENDIX 5a.

Situation B

Student Part one	Etudiant Première partie
You are in your office which is intolerably hot (or cold). You call the person responsible for the building's air-conditioning to inform him (her) of the situation.	Vous êtes dans votre bureau. Il y fait très chaud (ou très froid). Vous appelez la personne responsable de la climatisation dans l'édifice pour l'informer de la situation.
Part two	Deuxième partie
Your call is returned. You explain the problem of the unacceptable temperature in your office.	On vous retourne votre appel au sujet de la température de votre bureau. Vous exprimez vos idées à ce sujet.

APPENDIX 5b.

Situation B. Indications à l'examinateur.

Rôles: La scène se passe au bureau.

. *L'étudiant garde son identité. Il parle au téléphone d'abord à l'adjoint du responsable des services de climatisation dans l'édifice, puis au responsable lui-même.*

. Vous (l'examinateur) êtes d'abord l'adjoint, puis le responsable des services.

Attitude:

Assez hostile de la part de l'étudiant.
Conciliatrice de la part de l'adjoint et du responsable.

Déroulement:

Première partie

. *L'étudiant appelle le responsable des services de climatisation dans l'édifice.*

. Vous êtes son adjoint: vous dites que le responsable est absent et qu'il sera de retour dans quelques jours. Vous l'incitez à parler sur ces points.

. *Il vous décrit la température qu'il fait dans son bureau (trop chaud - trop froid - au choix)*

. *Il fait toutes sortes de commentaires au sujet de cette situation.*

. *Il vous demande de transmettre le message à quelqu'un d'autre.*

. *Vu que vous ne pouvez le faire, il insiste pour que vous transmettiez le message au responsable dès son retour.*

. Durant ce temps vous avez alimenté cette conversation en disant que vous ne pouvez pas prendre de décisions touchant la vérification des appareils de climatisation, que vous comprenez la situation, que seul votre patron est responsable des services et que vous lui transmettrez le message dès qu'il sera de retour.

Duexième partie

. Vous (le responsable des services) êtes de retour, vous rappelez l'étudiant.

. *L'étudiant commente la situation.*

. Vous le rassurez et discutez avec lui pour enfin conclure à la satisfaction de tous.

Summary of Scoring Criteria for Each Item

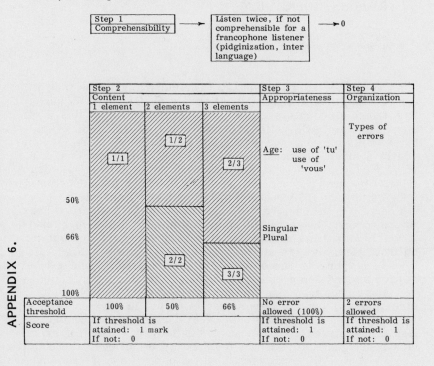

APPENDIX 6.

CREDIT RECOMMENDATIONS FOR ORAL PROFICIENCY

Douglas R. Whitney
American Council on Education

As a preface to my remarks, I should explain how it is that the American Council on Education (ACE) Office on Educational Credit and Credentials comes to be represented on this workshop agenda. ACE is the nation's major organization of colleges, universities, and education associations; there are currently nearly 1700 members. In general, ACE coordinates a variety of programs and projects of interest to many institutions. We also serve in an advisory capacity to colleges and universities on many matters of educational interest.

The ACE Office on Educational Credit and Credentials has, for more than 40 years, been evaluating the learning gained through formal instruction and informal study by persons not on campuses, judging the degree to which these skills and proficiencies relate to the outcomes of contemporary college-level study, and advising college officials as to the appropriateness of college credit awards for the completion of noncollegiate instruction and for the demonstration of proficiency on relevant tests. Each of the thousands of ACE credit recommendations issued to date is based on an evaluation by a panel of experienced college faculty drawn from campuses all over the country. In this role, ACE reviewers have an opportunity to conduct on-site reviews of military, government, and industry education programs that are not feasible for faculty from any particular campus. Test reviews bring faculty to our offices for one or more days of review and discussion.

In a soon-to-come day when adults are expected to represent a majority of undergraduate students in our colleges, it seems essential to offer sound means for recognizing and rewarding proficiency developed elsewhere. ACE has long maintained that college-level credit should be awarded for relevant demonstrated proficiency. Written tests, such as those

developed by the College-Level Examination Program (CLEP),
have been used for this purpose for more than a decade. It
is the judgment of our faculty reviewers that oral assessment
techniques, such as those used by the Foreign Service Institute, can be similarly useful. I hope that my remarks and the
subsequent report on the ACE credit recommendations serve to
stimulate wider use of tests of language proficiency in developing rewards for outstanding achievement by our students.

Since 1945, ACE faculty panels have evaluated instruction
offered by the military services. More than 75 percent of the
colleges in the United States use these recommendations as a
basis for credit awards.[1] Since 1974, ACE faculty panels have
evaluated instruction offered by businesses and by government
and volunteer agencies. About 45 percent of the colleges
nationwide use these recommendations in evaluating noncollegiate learning of adult students.[2]

After World War II, ACE college-level Tests of General Educational Development and the United States Armed Forces Institute (USAFI) Subject Standardized Tests enabled thousands of
returning service personnel to receive credit in four broad
areas of undergraduate general education studies and in specific college-level courses. In 1964, ACE recommendations for
credit helped launch the College Board College-Level Examination Program (CLEP) series and contributed to its wide acceptance. Since 1978, ACE has evaluated more than 120 separate
tests and assessment procedures as a part of a continuing program of test reviews.

Recently, James Frith, Dean of the Foreign Service Institute
School of Language Studies, asked us to constitute faculty
review panels for Spanish and French oral proficiency ratings
('S-ratings') as conducted at the Foreign Service Institute.
We are now completing these reviews. Our review guidelines
list a number of specific criteria that were addressed.[3] The
two basic questions, however, were: Are the skills tested relevant to college-level study? Are the procedures technically
sound? I will not attempt to summarize our panels' findings;
summaries of their reports will be available from ACE. Our
panels were generally enthusiastic and encouraged ACE to
issue credit recommendations in this area.

The ACE Commission on Educational Credit and Credentials
plans within the near future to issue advisory recommendations
to colleges and universities urging that varying amounts of
lower level undergraduate credit be awarded to persons tested
at the Foreign Service Institute if they achieve S-2 levels or
higher in the assessment. Since the skills reflected in the
Foreign Service Institute S-ratings are those generally empha-
sized in a four-semester introductory college course sequence,
the amounts of credit will range from six to twelve semester
hours. I should stress that these recommendations are advisory only, since credit awards are properly an institutional
and faculty responsibility.

In spite of a generally favorable evaluation of the Foreign Service Institute oral proficiency assessment procedures, I should note three problems encountered in our reviews; each influenced the nature of our advisory recommendations. Each arises from difficulty in standardizing enough aspects of the oral assessment procedure to draw legitimate and reliable inferences about a student's oral proficiency level. If college faculty are trained to conduct interviews along the lines of those used by the Foreign Service Institute, I foresee major procedural, interviewer, and standardization problems.

1. Foreign Service Institute testing evolved to meet one set of needs (State Department job qualification) and was not built specifically for use in qualifying for college credit. As a result, the skills tested in the FSI assessment are not quite what college faculty might have developed for the latter purpose. The skills tested are important and are among those generally stressed in college courses; the FSI S-ratings, however, do not directly reflect such commonly taught skills as reading and writing. Accordingly, our initial recommendations will not exceed the amounts for four semester introductory sequences; some institutions may wish to restrict these amounts or to require additional local testing to confirm credit awards. Too, some adaptations are clearly required in order for the content of the Foreign Service Institute interviews to be appropriate for college students aged 17 to 20.

2. A far more serious problem--in fact, a major reservation we have in issuing credit recommendations--is that there is no adequate set of norms to identify the levels of oral proficiency exhibited by current college students. In order to be very useful to college and university faculty, such norms must be gathered. Particularly important are the distributions of S-rating levels exhibited by students completing 1, 2, 3, and 4 semesters of introductory college-level language courses and by language majors at graduation. This absence of useful data is especially important at rating Levels S-1 and S-1+, and at levels above S-3. As a result, our recommendations are intended to be conservative at both ends of the scale and will be valid for only five years. We trust that better data will be available when we reevaluate the recommendations in 1985.

3. At present, most persons tested at the Foreign Service Institute already have college degrees, and there is little need for credit recommendations. Credit possibilities become viable only when the interviews can be conducted by campus faculty. We are persuaded that faculty participants in the two recent Foreign Service Institute workshops can conduct interviews in such a way as to yield results consistent with those of the Foreign Service Institute staff. But the clear definitions of each S-level can be easily distorted in meaning

by persons not so trained. There is currently no established mechanism for insuring consistency in the meaning of the ratings awarded by college faculty. Although we are enthusiastic about the possible uses on campuses, we will not encourage credit awards for any other oral proficiency systems until quality and consistency controls are in place. Specifically, we will extend our recommendations beyond the assessments conducted by the Foreign Service Institute staff only when the Foreign Service Institute certifies interviewers and examiners and when ratings are reported as an 'official' Foreign Service Institute report. We will do so automatically, however, when these controls are accomplished.

As were the Foreign Service workshop participants, our panels were enthusiastic about the potential of oral proficiency testing in many areas of language instruction in American higher education. To realize these valuable potentials requires: (1) the self-education, good judgment, and enthusiastic support of college and high school language faculty; (2) the establishment of an official agency to train and certify interviewers, to monitor interview samples to insure consistency, and to issue 'official' results and reports that can be recognized as a standardized source of proficiency ratings; and (3) the routine collection and updating of normative and interpretive data on the proficiency levels of relevant samples of contemporary college students.

To accomplish these ends, you must move together in observable ways to recognize and reward students' oral proficiency. Some agency has to ensure the kind of standardization that enables interested persons to infer similar levels of proficiency from different interviews and interview procedures. This seems to be an area characterized by a number of enthusiastic followers with no clear leader.

The extensive use of oral proficiency assessment techniques in college credit-by-examination and placement programs and in occupational licensing programs seems to await only the emergence of a resourceful leader to assume the responsibilities and resolve the problems I have noted here. Who will that agency, organization, or person be?

NOTES

1. *The 1978 Guide to the Evaluation of Educational Experiences in the Armed Services.* Washington, D.C.: American Council on Education.

2. *The National Guide to Educational Credit for Training Programs.* Washington, D.C.: American Council on Education, 1980.

3. Copies of the general review guidelines used in the ACE test review program are available from the author.

ON USING FOREIGN SERVICE INSTITUTE TESTS AND STANDARDS ON CAMPUSES

Howard T. Young
Pomona College

In the spring of 1978, the Modern Language Association/ American Council of Learned Societies Task Force on Institutional Policy released a report that contained nearly a score of innovative and important recommendations. The keystone recommendation, the one on which, in the opinion of Richard Brod, all others must depend, had to do with the need to identify, more clearly than is now generally done, proficiency standards for students learning a foreign language. Such standards would obviously need to be implemented by an evaluation system, and, accordingly, Recommendation Number 10 of the Task Force reads:

> Institutions and, where appropriate, state educational systems should be encouraged ... to adopt nationally recognized performance or proficiency standards and make such standards widely known to students, faculty, and the public.

Among the most prestigious and consistently successful tests with a detailed performance criteria standard and a highly controlled application is the famous Foreign Service Institute (FSI) oral interview. This proficiency examination has, since its inception in 1956, sent some 60,000 State Department and other government employees communicating in some 60 languages around the world with a recognized, readily definable proficiency label of S-1, S-2, etc. In addition, under the supervision of the Educational Testing Service (ETS), the FSI examination has been used to certify a large number of Peace Corps volunteers.

The remarkable accomplishment of the oral proficiency interview is attributable to many factors: tight organization, quality control, classes that teach to it, continuous feedback from the field, and, most of all, ambitious, motivated, articulate students.

For the language profession as a whole, here was a model worth looking at, a proficiency test with widely recognized and accepted performance criteria. The questions to be asked were: (1) Did it have any applicability outside the umbrella of FSI? (2) Could it survive in the bewildering diversity of standards at American colleges and universities?

In order to discover some answers to these questions, FSI convened in February, 1979 a two-day workshop of 12 participants from colleges and universities around the country. These language teachers heard a rationale for the criteria, watched the examination being administered, learned the scoring technique, and began to conduct interviews themselves. After the two-day period, they went back to their campuses, administered interviews to approximately 20 students, and compared the scores assigned with those given by seasoned FSI examiners. Final agreement between faculty testers and FSI interviewers reached 96 percent, which would indicate that the testing procedure could be readily taught in a reasonable amount of time. [1]

A second workshop was organized in January, 1980 with 19 participants. Plans are under way for a third and fourth workshop.

The academic response was initially one of polite attention; but it soon turned respectful as the test was analyzed, and appreciation grew as the professors learned how to conduct and rate their own examinations. Back on campus in contact with students, the response of the involved academicians has been enthusiastic. Students have cooperated eagerly and colleagues have on the whole joined in with alacrity.

On the basis of the experience of members of the first workshop, we are in a position to report briefly about some current uses at colleges and universities of the FSI examination, indicate proposed uses, and point out some of its limitations as the academic community sees them.

An example of incorporation into classroom procedures has occurred at Brigham Young University. The French department has trained advanced peers and native speakers to administer a modified and shortened form of the oral interview. The examination will be given every other week over a period of three semesters. Students receive feedback throughout. At the end of the three-year period, plans call for administration of a full-fledged FSI examination to the approximately 100 students involved. Information will eventually be produced to show correlation between oral tests and overall grade.

This is perhaps the most extensive use currently being made in the classroom of the testing techniques learned at FSI, but all of the members of the workshop have used it informally to test advanced classes: at Ohio State, the examination helped

evaluate teaching assistants; San Antonio College employed it
as an adjunct to placement tests; Pomona College used it to
examine informally applicants for the semester abroad program
in Spain. Portland State Oregon developed a testing team in
Spanish, French, and German and took steps to incorporate
the exam into their advanced classes. They are working on
establishing an appropriate exit score at this level. Fulbright
applicants from Portland are now administered the FSI test, as
are all students receiving a Master of Arts in English as a
Second Language. In addition, this industrious department
tested applicants who scored in the 90th percentile in the
American Association of Teachers of German high school con-
test, thereby supplying an additional element of evaluation.
It is expected that a state commission on foreign language
study, to be convened by the governor, will take considerable
interest in the oral proficiency examination. At Georgetown
University, the test was demonstrated to the combined faculty
of the School of Languages and Linguistics. Finally, hundreds
of college students were given the full-length FSI examination
by several workshop participants as part of ETS's Global
Awareness Project. Growing familiarity with the examination
led a number of faculty members to foresee wide and impres-
sive uses of an oral proficiency test along the lines of the FSI
model.

There is general agreement among the participants in the
first FSI workshop that the oral interview could be used pretty
much in its present form as a part of an exit requirement for
foreign language majors at the Bachelor of Arts level. Tran-
scripts of University A, College B, State College C would con-
tain, in addition to the usual list of language and literature
courses with the traditional letter grades, the rating on oral
proficiency. If this rating is based on nationally recognized
criteria and standards, such a label would announce more
effectively than anything now available the oral skills of the
language major.

Pomona College is considering a plan whereby its majors in
International Relations would be required to display their
speaking proficiency through a bona fide version of the FSI
test. Eventually, in many colleges and universities, one
would hope to provide certificates of speaking proficiency for
majors other than those in foreign languages.

It seems logical and feasible to use the examination to certify
teaching assistants in graduate schools. This cadre of tyro
language teachers, some of whom may be uncertain in their
oral skills, would be significantly strengthened in the process,
and the result would, in turn, fortify university language programs, for it is well known that at large schools the entire
undergraduate teaching of languages is placed in the hands of
these individuals.

Quite clearly, as usage of the oral interview spreads, it
will have repercussions on the classroom. Experience with the

Advanced Placement Program in high schools shows that, if there is a national test, classes and teachers will teach to it. Should the oral interview become common, students will soon be engaging in mini-interviews in the classroom. Already, however, in most languages, there is enough emphasis on oral skills so that no basic revision of classroom procedures is likely to be required.

The examination in its present form can be a valuable instrument for evaluating semester abroad programs. What is the average score of a student with one semester of study abroad as opposed to two, the score of a student who lives in a dorm as opposed to a home?

Nearly everyone agrees that wider use should be made of the examination for the certification of high school teachers. This already occurs in some states (for example, California), but it should be, in the opinion of many workshop participants, a mandatory component of the state board examination.

Use of the oral test for credit by examination is an area in which the American Council on Education intends to make positive recommendations in the near future.

A bold idea is the suggestion to establish a reasonable oral proficiency level (perhaps S-1) for the fulfillment of the language requirement. Here is a stunning example of the improvement in articulation that widely accepted standards would generate. A requirement for oral proficiency often rendered meaningless by the diversity of standards not only throughout the country but sometimes within the same institutions or departments could be examined against a hard set of widely publicized criteria.

Once universities produce students trained along the lines of clearly defined proficiencies, prospective employers can confidently screen for language ability in their applicants. This has significant applications for language students in relation to the job market.

Those members of the profession involved in the FSI workshops have responded with unanimous enthusiasm to Recommendation Number 10 of the MLA Task Force on Institutional Policy: 'It will put an end to the "Balkanization" of language teaching', 'It will make us accountable', 'It is the most exciting task facing foreign language teachers in the 1980s', are typical comments.

Nevertheless, a caveat has been issued. We are warned to move slowly and carefully in seeking acceptance of national standards. If it is made a question of quality and prestige, most people will gradually go along; if too much external pressure is exerted, the vein of anarchy in the American academic tradition will be intensified.

High on the list of recommendations, in fact, the heart of the issue, is the need for a quality control vested in some kind of certification board. Currently, this function is handled by FSI and ETS, but a way of regionalizing it and perhaps,

through the Association of Departments of Foreign Languages,
or the American Council on the Teaching of Foreign Languages,
Inc., placing it in the hands of certain departments, must be
devised. Clearly, no one can certify on his own; ideally,
successful completion of a course will one day be the only
certification needed.

There are several things that the FSI oral proficiency test
does not do. For one, in the matter of evaluation, the grada-
tions are perhaps not fine enough to replace currently used
academic achievement grades. We need correlation studies between the traditional A B C D F and the S-0 to S-5. In the
meantime, we know that the oral examination is not a face valid
test of such skills as reading, writing, culture, sense of style,
and appreciation of literature. In a good language class, the
student becomes aware of how a language functions; he acquires
some conscious sense of the linguistic process, analyzes, in-
duces, and deduces. In addition, he encounters aspects of
the culture in its most communicable form: language. This is
a rich gamut of experience that the academic community,
especially quality liberal arts colleges, will want to quantify
more carefully in light of working with tests like the FSI model.

In its present form the FSI interview takes 20 to 40 minutes
to complete and requires two people to administer it: an interviewer and an examiner. Wide application of this format would
require radical adjustments in teaching staff at all institutions;
and in a time of economic stringencies in academe, such adjustments are unlikely to occur. The profession will need, therefore, to consider modifications of the FSI oral interview and to
entertain the notion of shortening it considerably. It should
be able to do this and still maintain a detailed description of
performance at every level that will serve as a national yard-
stick.

Finally, in the as yet gargantuan task of publicity and education within the profession, it is essential that we address
our high school colleagues. This is the level at which Ameri-
ca's language 'crisis', to refer to the term used by the Presi-
dential Commission, can in the long run be most effectively resolved. It has been suggested that state foreign language
coordinators be invited to workshops in order to allow them
the opportunity of experiencing first-hand the FSI procedures.

Meanwhile, Karl Schevill at the School of Education at Berke-
ley is working on training secondary teachers of French, German, and Spanish to administer brief oral examinations to their
students. The examination is miniscule compared to that of the
FSI and its standards require fine tuning, but the goal is ad-
mirable. Currently, the University of California requires for
admission a high school foreign language experience at Level 2.
What does Level 2 mean? Karl Schevill and his team of PEFLers
(Performance Evaluation in FL) propose to answer that question.

As work proceeds apace on the development of nationally recognized performance standards for the speaking of foreign languages, one is tempted to think ahead to a period 10 years from now when the profession is liable to ask: how did we ever get along without a clearly defined set of proficiency standards? How did we manage to test without a hard set of widely accepted criteria to refer to? How did we survive so long teaching the most universal of disciplines while depending almost entirely on what, no matter how well handled, was an essentially provincial diagnosis?

NOTES

In the preparation of this report I would like to acknowledge the assistance of Dean James R. Frith of the Foreign Service Institute and my colleagues of FSI Testing Kit Workshop Number One: Roger Bensky (Georgetown University), Therese Bonin (Ohio State University), Thomas Brown (Brigham Young University), William Cressey (Georgetown University), Louis J. Elteto (Portland State University), Gerard Ervin (Ohio State University), David Gobert (Southern Illinois University), Phyllis Johnson (Pomona College), Howard Lamson (Earlham College), John Rassias (Dartmouth College), William Samelson (San Antonio College).

1. For further details concerning the workshop, see James R. Frith, 'Testing the FSI Testing Kit', ADFL 11 November, 1979, pp. 12-14.